T0318836

HOW TO USE BOOKS

HOW TO USE BOOKS

by

LIONEL McCOLVIN

LONDON
PUBLISHED FOR
THE NATIONAL BOOK LEAGUE
BY CAMBRIDGE UNIVERSITY PRESS

CAMBRIDGE
UNIVERSITY PRESS

University Printing House, Cambridge CB2 8BS, United Kingdom

Cambridge University Press is part of the University of Cambridge.

It furthers the University's mission by disseminating knowledge in the pursuit of
education, learning and research at the highest international levels of excellence.

www.cambridge.org
Information on this title: www.cambridge.org/9781316612002

© Cambridge University Press 1947

First published 1933
Second edition 1947
Reprinted 1948
First paperback edition 2016

A catalogue record for this publication is available from the British Library

ISBN 978-1-316-61200-2 Paperback

CONTENTS

CHAPTER ONE

INTRODUCTION

MEN, of the author's generation, who served in the war of 1914-18 will remember how, when they were in training, they used to practise 'passing messages'. It was a pleasant and amusing change from more strenuous drill. They would spread out a few feet apart, so as not to overhear one another, and then the instructor, speaking quietly, gave the nearest man a 'message' – a short and simple sentence. The first man told the second, the second the third, and so on to the end.

The last man *should* have received exactly the same message as the first, but, as often as not, he didn't. It was surprising how the original sentence would get distorted, even though it passed through but a dozen mouths and ears. Words would be missed out. Words would be added. Words would have changed their meaning, sound and significance, be altered, even reversed.

Although these recruits were trying to keep the message intact and accurate they often failed. How if they had been excited or unheeding? What would the percentage of error have been then? Try it, as a parlour game, and see.

There is the well-known instance – obviously untrue, yet illustrating the point – of the officer who was about to attack. He 'passed' a message asking the captain of the neighbouring company for assistance. None came, and he wondered why, until he learned later that the captain had received no message at all that morning excepting this, which he took for a joke – 'I am going to a dance. Can you lend me three and fourpence?' It is easy to guess the original message. 'I am going to advance. Can you send me reinforcements?'

If that might happen with a few men in a few minutes,

ask yourself how accurate, how complete, your knowledge of things in general would be if all the information you had on every matter, beyond the few things you could see for yourself, had had to come to you by word of mouth, from hundreds of mouths, uttering strange languages, perhaps speaking down the centuries, across the world. And it would be tainted and transformed, not only because it had not been 'heard' properly, but also because every man who carried it a step nearer to you would receive it and send it forth again according to his own knowledge and personality. In such circumstances you would not, if you had any alternative, rely overmuch on its accuracy.

Neither would your information be complete.

Think how much you forget, even though you want to remember it. If a thing is at all important you have to *make a note of it*.

Consider our knowledge of past times – of, say, the Middle Ages. Students may, by a process of conjecture, comparison, and piecing together, be able to reconstruct the life of the times and give us, in general terms, a fair idea of conditions. But what actual *facts* have come down to us – facts which are unassailable and definite? The names and ordinances of kings and chiefs, the decrees of popes and priests, the decisions of courts of law – those matters, in brief, which have been put down in black and white. Practically everything else has been forgotten. Thousands of years of human history have had to be written round a few notes jotted down by the way. Of the personal history of some of our greatest men – for example, Shakespeare – we know little but what has been dug up from legal documents relating to leases, sales of property, disputes, and the like, from registers, and from the odd occasions when friends and contemporaries mentioned them in their letters and writings.

By *writing* alone can we transmit information from one generation to another, unless the actual things that people make – buildings, coins, statues, tools – themselves survive, and even then we don't always know what they are unless there is some written explanation.

Even that is not all.

If you were engaged on scientific research and you had to begin right at the beginning, finding out everything for yourself, ignorant of what previous scientists had learned, unable to compare notes with other workers in different parts of the world, how far would you get in a lifetime?

One could ask many similar questions. We have only to give the matter a few moments' consideration to realize that, after the discovery of how to make fire and after the gradual development of speech by which men might exchange their thoughts and ideas, the most important factor in human history was the invention and perfection of means by which speech might be recorded – writing and, later, printing.

It meant that, for the first time, it was possible, in a world of change and confusion, to pick out a fact and 'nail it down' for all time, unchanging, unambiguous – to say: 'This is' or 'This was', so that all might know.

It meant that a man could communicate with those with whom he could not speak – either because they were far away or because they were not yet born.

It meant that each generation could hand on something of what it had learned; that each generation started a little further ahead; that gradually we *accumulated* knowledge and power.

It meant – a point of no less importance – that a man did not need to rely only on what he knew himself. There is a limit, which is very soon reached, to what anyone can remember and understand. Before writing came no one *could* know more than he himself and his neighbours were able to learn and remember. It could only be a very small part of the sum total of knowledge. Once writing was invented, however, once manuscripts and books were accessible, it became possible to *find out*.

So we may assert that our present-day civilization owes

its existence to the written word, the printed page. If to-morrow we all forgot how to read, in a very few years we should have reverted to the conditions of the Dark Ages – if, indeed, we survived the chaos that would ensue.

Books form only a small part of the total output of printed matter. Millions of different items, all designed to convey or record information, are circulated every year – handbills, price-lists, catalogues, programmes, and the like, the reports and minutes of thousands of institutions and organizations, newspapers, periodicals, maps, plans, time-tables, prospec-tuses, calendars, leaflets, and pamphlets of every description.

Here, however, we are concerned only with books – the most substantial, the most permanent and in some ways the most important of printed publications.

How many books are there in the world? It is impossible to say, but the following figures will give some slight indication:

Since the invention of printing many million different books have been published. Of some of them hundreds of different editions have been issued and millions of copies sold. Think of the enormous circulations of such books as the Bible, Shakespeare's or Molière's works, The Pilgrim's Progress, and many others, often much less famous.

Before the war 17,000 *different* new books and new editions were published in one year in Great Britain alone, a similar number in Japan, nearly twice as many in pre-Nazi Germany, 7000 in the United States – and other countries more or less in proportion. The number fell con-siderably during the war; the total for Great Britain in 1944 was only 6781. Once conditions become normal again, how-ever, we are likely to exceed the pre-war output because there is a considerable accumulation of interesting and im-portant books the publication of which waits only until more labour and material are available.

How many copies of each book are sold we do not know, but remember that practically every copy is read by several people. If it is sold to a circulating library it might be read by a hundred or two before it is finally discarded. Moreover, books are kept – some for only a short while, as their interest is passing, but others for tens and even hundreds of years. In other words, this stupendous output of books becomes an accumulation, an ever-increasing asset.

Consequently, since all sorts and conditions of men are reading, and reading about the things which interest and help them most, we find that the world of books covers an immense field – one almost as extensive as life itself. There are few trades, shades of political opinion, religious beliefs, hobbies, nationalities, which are not represented even in the list of periodicals published regularly, and when we turn to books we should all find it exceedingly difficult, if not impossible, to name any subject about which a book has not been written at some time or other.

If you were to study the contents of a large general library you would find an entire world in little. There would be books recording everything at all significant, important, interesting, usual or unusual, that men had ever seen, done, experienced, thought, or imagined.

As a rule libraries are 'classified' – arranged so that all books on the same or similar subjects are brought together. This arrangement is necessary for many reasons but, by bringing 'order' into what would otherwise be chaos, it makes it less easy to grasp at once the enormous *variety* of the material. This factor would be more apparent if we went into a library that was *not* classified, for there we should find a strange assortment of books – serious and trivial, accurate and utterly unreliable, attractive and dull, ahead of public opinion and completely out of date. Books in which great men seek to help their fellows to attain happiness, books on how to manufacture poison-gas, lives of kings and treatises on bee-keeping, sermons and Acts of Parliament, books about geography, geology, music, psychology and similar familiar themes, and books about vector analysis, curvilinear motion, geraniaceæ, anticlisis, and thousands of other such subjects, the very titles of which would mean nothing to most of us, would jostle one another on the shelves.

Yet, innumerable though the themes themselves might be, there is still another factor which increases the multiplicity and variety of books – the reader and his special needs. He may know nothing about a particular subject or he may know nearly everything; he may be studying it in order to pass an examination; he may be interested only in a general way in its most interesting features; he may be of exceptional intelligence, or he may be barely able to read at all. He may, in fact, approach it in any of a hundred ways. And the book written for one would be useless to another, although the 'subject' is the same. So the book world must cater for all these needs.

Consequently, if you want to get some idea of the extent of literature you should think, first, of all the conceivable subjects you can remember, and then imagine books written so as to please everyone who might have any need to read about them. Add a few million for stories, poems, plays and other 'imaginative' books . . . and does anyone now dare to say that there aren't *some* books that he himself ought to read?

Unfortunately, only those whose lives are spent with books – librarians, booksellers, research-workers and the like – have any conception of their amazing range and variety. The average man only knows a few types – shall we say, perhaps the detective story, the time-table and the Bible, or the school text, the practical handbook and poetry. Most of us live in a world full of useful, interesting books, but we do not realize it. We have a few friends when we might have many; only one or two literary assistants when we might call upon an army of helpers.

The objects of this little book therefore are to indicate something of the scope and variety of books, to show how, whatever your interests and circumstances may be, they can be of some use to you, and, which is equally important, to help you to discover and obtain those you require.

So long as a man has access to books there are very few matters about which he cannot learn something. Reading alone does not suffice. Knowledge and information only become of any value when they are applied to some human end, when they lead to better accomplishment or keener understanding. Yet – in spite of what militant 'men of action' might preach – the great needs of the present generation (as of all past generations too) are on the one hand more, and more accurate, facts regarding all phases of activity, and, on the other, a brighter vision, a keener imagination. Both of these needs may, to a large extent, be supplied by reading.

To bring this still nearer home – it may safely be asserted that whoever the reader ·may be, whatever his occupation, whatever his circumstances, if, by means of books, he keeps himself in touch with all that is most significant in life and fully informed on all matters concerning his own personal activities, he will surely be much more successful than others with similar ability and good fortune who *neglect* books. And if the reader should have 'bad fortune', he will probably learn, from those same books, that 'success' is not everything, and that the worst of ill-luck has its compensations.

The use of books has increased greatly during and since the war. New books have been in such demand that many have been unobtainable a few days after publication – a condition arising partly from the limitation of supplies but also from increased desire to read and ability to buy. For example, shortly before the end of hostilities the first edition of a book by an eminent historian, on a theme of wide appeal, was exhausted before publication; the edition was not, however, a small one – in fact it was much larger than any first printing of any of that author's books in prewar days. To continue – the prices of second-hand books have soared. The work of public libraries throughout has been from twenty to fifty per cent greater than in 1939.

For this war-time renaissance in reading there are many reasons. On the one hand, people had fewer opportunities for other recreations, more cause to stay at home, new opportunities for reading – as, for example, when 'standing-by' for civil defence duties, a greater need for relaxation and 'escape'. On the other hand, people had new things to do and new problems to solve, about all of which they needed information and guidance. Above all people were intensely eager to know more and to think more wisely about the world in which they lived, about the forces that had brought civilization so near to disaster and about the ways in which the future could be made more secure and fruitful.

With the return of peace some of the purely war-time factors, such as 'black-out' and 'stand-by', have ceased to operate but the main influences continue. Men and women who have once acquired the habit of reading and thus come to appreciate its value, seldom cease to read. The new readers were not all civilians, either. Tens of thousands in the Navy, Army and Air Force have started to read – so much so, indeed, that the many millions of books distributed by the Services Central Book Depot, the Services' education departments and other large scale agencies proved quite insufficient to satisfy the demand.

In brief, the number of readers in the post-war world will be many more than ever before. And the moral is obvious: in a book-using civilization the man who does not use them places himself at a grave disadvantage compared with his fellows.

CHAPTER TWO

THE BOOKS YOU WANT

NOWHERE in this book is it suggested that you should *ever* read unless you gain *some* benefit – recreational or informative – from reading – or if you would be better occupied doing anything else.

This might sound very lukewarm recommendation of books; but it isn't. If you utilize *all* your opportunities for *useful* reading you will be well occupied.

Book use might be divided into three types: Firstly, *purposive use*, when you read or consult or study books with some definite object in mind, such as gathering information for a debate or learning how to do something which you propose to undertake, and so on – book use which is directly associated with your various other activities. Secondly, there is *reading for interest* and stimulation – when you read books because they are about things which interest you; because they add to your general store of knowledge and understanding, widen your range of appreciation, and generally broaden your outlook and help to 'educate' you. Thirdly, there is the mere pastime of reading – in which we are all more or less guilty of indulging – when we read, not because, when we have finished, we shall be any wiser or better, but simply because we want mental relaxation, because we are tired or, more likely, just lazy. There is nothing 'wrong' about such reading; but with a wider knowledge of books we can often select reading which belongs to the second category – which interests and stimulates – while still serving as excellent recreation.

Now ask yourself the question: 'What use can books be to *me?*'

With the first class of book use, the answer is: 'Whenever you have occasion to know anything you don't know, what-

ever the reason, whatever kind of information it might be.'
There is some information you cannot find in books; for
example, it might concern events of too recent occurrence;
it might be of too limited appeal; it might be 'private' (such
as a secret trade process); but it is surprising how much you
can find. Of course, you need to know something about
books and how to handle them before they are of the fullest
use; to discover the answers to *some* questions you have to
be a specialist in research work with a very wide knowledge
of the literature of your subject. You will soon, however,
acquire facility with practice, and generally you will have
little difficulty in satisfying *most* of your needs. Moreover,
at your libraries (and your bookshops in certain cases) you
will find qualified people always willing to help you – of
which more later.

Keep this in mind, then. If you want to know anything,
try books first.

Examples are probably unnecessary, but the following
instances will serve to remind some readers of possible uses
for books:

At work – to keep in touch with the best and newest
methods; to remedy defects and improve conditions; to find
solutions for problems of organization and administration;
to discover new markets and their special requirements; to
settle legal questions; to understand better the processes of
manufacture, the qualities and defects of raw materials; to
organize publicity campaigns; to understand financial
matters, banks and how to use them; to help fill up income
tax returns; arrange shop windows; learn book-keeping,
shorthand, filing methods, and so on. There are hundreds
of books on all these matters.

At home – to make or mend anything; to use your garden
to the best advantage, discovering what to plant and how to
look after it; to decorate, furnish, cope with minor ailments,
choose schools and careers for your children; arrange your
private affairs; care for dogs and keep pets; cook, manage
the household, entertain; to enjoy your hobby and pursue

it to advantage, perhaps with profit; to learn more about the music you hear, the things you collect, etc. etc.

If you travel for business or pleasure – where to go, the best routes, the times of trains and boats, what to look for en route, the best seasons; how to look after and repair your car, your bicycle, how to go camping.

How to do anything – why, when, what *not* to do.

And, of course, to answer all the usual 'Where is?' 'What is?' 'Who is?' 'How do I spell?' 'What does it mean?' questions you will have your few well-chosen books of reference at home also.

The second class of reading is even wider and no less important. It embraces the whole of imaginative literature and much more besides – all, indeed, that the 'inquiring mind' may seek in its desire for further wisdom and understanding and to satisfy that human instinct which has done more than any other to aid progress – curiosity.

It is unnecessary to discuss here the value of literature, as numerous books designed to assist the reader to enjoy the best of our poetry, fiction, plays and belles-lettres already exist. Sufficient to say that, apart from the intense satisfaction we derive from the beauty and felicity of expression when significant ideas are presented in the most effective manner, as they are in good literature, in studying the fine art of writing we come into contact with singularly alert and perceptive minds. Poets and essayists, novelists and playwrights, are not, as so often they are reputed to be, either dreamers and idealists out of touch with reality or writers concerned chiefly with perfection of expression. If they were we should have little use for them. Actually they are more likely to be men who write clearly and beautifully because they have *thought* clearly and intensely, men whose supposed remoteness from reality may only consist in ignoring the external, temporary and unimportant aspects in order that these may not obscure the essentials.

The chief appeal of imaginative literature is its *human* appeal; its chief value is its revelation of ourselves and others.

As has been said, however, there are many guides to this branch of 'interest reading'. The reader is much more likely to overlook the many ways books can be related to various *general* interests and sympathies. By reading, these interests themselves can be strengthened. A thousand instances might be given: For example, Mr. A had a general, vague and rather useless sense of sympathy for the slum-dweller (It might equally well have been the discharged prisoner or *any* type of unfortunate). He knew nothing definite about conditions or causes at first, when, by chance, he picked up a popular booklet on the subject. Actually this particular book was a very badly biased piece of propaganda, but it aroused his interest. He read other books and then others, until in time he was able to take an active part in solving a social problem to which, without this study, he could have contributed nothing.

Miss B's case is of a much different type. She went to the 'pictures' regularly, but simply to pass time, and she was bored more often than not. Then, again by accident, she came across a book on the theory of the cinema. It was a 'high-brow' production, mostly unintelligible and unpractical in the extreme, but it served to show Miss B that there was something more in the cinema than she had realized. Even the worst pictures, when viewed not merely as novelettes brought to life, afforded much material for intelligent questioning and criticism. More books were read – though, indeed, there are not many good books on this subject – and eventually her field of interest was widened beyond the cinema to its parent art, the stage drama, and she became, for the first time, a theatre-goer and a reader of printed plays. These companion studies and their inter-relations, together with an increasing appreciation of the art of the photographer, give Miss B full occupation for her leisure.

The striking feature of interest reading is this 'leading on' process. A course of non-purposive reading is not unlike a good conversation: it may start with immortality and end with the culture of sweetpeas or with washing bills, or it may be the other way round. And, as washing and sweet-peas and immortality are all part of the same all-embracing topic – life – it is fitting that in a conversation they should be related even by haphazard links to one another. The charm of conversation lies in this free wandering inconsequence.

In general reading the best method is that of following up each new line of thought as it is disclosed and pursuing it as long as its fascination holds or until a greater attraction is offered. To plan a course of reading beforehand is undesirable – unless, of course, you have a definite objective. If you say, 'I will read first this, then that, and then the other', you make reading a self-imposed duty rather than a compelling pleasure. Set off, instead, with an inquiring mind, resolved 'to get to the bottom of it', but without ever saying what 'it' is, and you will be happy. In reading there is always something round the corner.

How are *you* to know what you will enjoy until you meet with it?

Just one example of a reader's pilgrimage (as indicated by a list of books he had read): He evidently began with a pamphlet on the United Nations project, and the topics about which he next read were, in this order, the causes of war, the biology of war (the 'man is a pugnacious animal and is bound to keep on squabbling' idea), the social life of animals (to see if there was anything in the theory), the social life of primitive man, primitive religion and magic, the wanderings of prehistoric peoples, the archaeology of England, the old churches of England, the work of the craftsmen of the Middle Ages and their guilds. Now he is dipping into the works of William Morris and, probably, the cycle of his thoughts will take him next to socialism, thence to internationalism and so back to his starting-point. These literary explorations have a knack of running in circles, returning home at intervals, but pursuing their course without any conscious plan.

Our reader might not know a great deal about any of the themes he touched upon, but in the sum total of his inquiries he has learned much more than he would from any regular systematic course, since all the while he has read only because he wanted to find out more about the things which appealed most to him. As psychologists and educationists are well aware, we remember best those things we most *like* remembering.

Courses of study are not, of course, condemned. On the contrary, if you find a course which you can pursue to the bitter end without losing interest you will be well advised to gain the combined advantages of systematic reading and sustained enthusiasm. Similarly, if, through want of experience or because your circumstances make study difficult, you find it a help and an aid to concentration to have your route planned out beforehand, by all means adopt a course. Don't, however, commit yourself to *too* long a course or to one which is too advanced, and don't be perturbed if you find you want to fly off at a tangent and read something else.

One little matter might be mentioned in passing: Reference has been made to a 'list of books read'. Many readers keep such a record. It is very useful to people who read books which are so machine-made that their only distinguishing mark is the title; it prevents their wasting their time re-reading books which at the first reading made so little impression that they are now completely forgotten. It is quite bad enough to read them once. Otherwise there is little point in lists. You know what you have read and what you haven't, and if you keep a list there is always the danger of making a fetish of it – by finishing books you don't want to read simply in order to be able to enter them up. Quite a few *do* behave so stupidly.

But – and this will be discussed in a later chapter – whenever you make a note of anything, no matter what it is, always add to it the name and author of the book from which it is noted with its date and edition. You might want to use or to follow up and amplify your notes and unless you know the source the notes are useless.

To refer again to 'interest reading'. Occasions when books can make the other things you do more interesting are innumerable, if you will only look for them. As there will be, it is hoped, some who read this book who have not yet begun to use books fully, here are a few suggestions as to how the first steps might best be taken. You – those of you who are on the threshold of the book world – probably read novels of a fairly popular character, scan the newspapers, and occupy your time with some form of work and a hobby or two.

Let these – your novels, newspapers, work and hobbies – be your starting-point. Is there anything you enjoy that you could enjoy better with the help of books? Is there anything you do that you could do better with books? Do you ever feel that your curiosity is aroused, that you would like to know more about this or that, but you don't quite know how to satisfy your interest? Yesterday you wouldn't have bothered. You would have said: 'I wonder . . .' 'Why should . . .?' 'Is that true?' 'How can that be?' And left it at that. To-day you cease to be content. You try to find out. You realize now that all the loose ends *can* be sorted out and tied up, if only you take a little trouble. You know now that you can't leave the matter so imperfectly explained, and that, if you turn to books, there is no excuse to remain uninformed. Yours is an 'inquiring' mind, and you use it.

Novels make a good starting-point. Truth is stranger than fiction. A story, to interest you, must be based upon real life; it must tell you of the doings of men and women very like men and women who have really lived; the experiences they endure must be very much the same as the real experiences of flesh and blood people. Why not turn from fiction to fact?

It is a sea story – of shipwrecks, of piracy, of exploration. Real men have been wrecked; there were real pirates; the world has been explored, opened out, and described by real men. Why not read about *them*? Why not read their own accounts of their lives?

It is a love story. What about some of the great romances of real life – of the Brownings, Lincoln, Robert Louis Stevenson, Nelson, Victor Hugo, Berlioz, and a thousand more?

It is a tale with a Canadian, or a Chinese, or a Swiss setting. You enjoy reading about life in these countries and about the scenery as part of the background of a romance or story of adventure. Accounts of travel in these lands will probably prove no less fascinating.

It is an historical novel. Clearly a cleverly written book on some period – not a dull textbook, but one of the many attempts to make the past real and vital – will be very much the same thing. You might even enjoy it more because, probably, your liking for historical novels is due to your interest in olden times and your fondness for romance and action as much as to the appeal of 'just a story'.

Even the detective yarn has its real life counterpart.

In short, the stuff from which novels are made is the stuff of life – of real life. So why not, for a change, find it at first hand? This journey from fiction to fact will not only widen your interest; it will also help to make more enjoyable whatever novels you may read in the future. The more you can contribute to a book, the more you get out of it. For example, should you encounter a story set in your native county, when the characters live in places you yourself have seen, when the author describes familiar beauty spots, don't you enjoy it more than if it had all happened in a strange and unknown locality? Know something of the people, conditions, times and places, and you enjoy the novel better.

Another line of approach is provided by the author. What sort of a man was he? Did he himself experience any adventures similar to those he describes in his stories? How did he gain his knowledge of mankind? Did he himself know joys and sorrows like those of his characters? Perhaps there is a biography of him which will tell you.

Newspaper reading raises a thousand questions in the inquiring mind. You read of events in all parts of the world, concerning phases of existence that may be totally different from anything you have experienced. If you are honest you will admit that there are columns and columns that you can't really understand. At least you don't know enough about the matters discussed to form any useful judgment. You can't all be experts and you don't need to be, but you should be able to appreciate the general significance and meaning of news when it is presented impartially and to recognize when it isn't. This is not an attack upon newspapers. It is an attack upon *you* – if you expect too much from the daily press. Newspapers are like every other kind of influence. What you get from them depends on what you bring to them.

You must not expect the newspapers to be a popular educator complete and all-sufficing in penny numbers. That isn't their job. Their function is to provide you with the latest chapters of books you are supposed to have read from the beginning elsewhere; to tell you the most recent happenings; not what has gone before to cause those happenings. *That* you must find out for yourselves by reading.

If you regard them as pure entertainment, as a means of whiling away a railway journey, if you don't yourself think about the 'news', if you aren't willing to regard critically the events of your own day, if you are not prepared to try and sort out the important and significant things from the superficial and know why and how they are significant, how can you expect to play an intelligent part as a citizen of a democratic nation? Yet, undoubtedly, it is your duty to do so. To an ever-increasing extent the affairs of the world are, for good or ill, governed by the opinions of ordinary men and women. Unless these opinions are based upon a reasonable and knowledgeable interest you mustn't expect much from democracy. Therefore if any phase of current events should appeal to you, if any item of news should drive home to you your absolute ignorance of its main features, follow it up, not by making a task of it, but by finding readable books covering the ground in a popular manner.

Such reading will help you to be critical, providing the facts and ideas with which to check the newspapers' presentation of events and movements – both the things they tell and the things they omit to tell. We are not suggesting that your newspaper this morning, or any day, is deliberately trying to delude you. That may be unlikely – but it is for *you* to judge. And you'll be very unwise to forget that the recent war would never have happened if large numbers of ordinary people, in certain countries, had *not* allowed themselves to be misled.

Next is your work – another unlimited field. You will, of course, have realized that whatever you do you must study if you would get on, that you must be better informed, more up to date than your competitors. So there is no need to urge you to continue your purely professional or business reading. We are thinking here rather of 'interest' reading that will combine business with pleasure. Your work is bound to link on to some themes about which books have been written. If you are engaged in trade or commerce – how are the things you deal in made? Whence do they come? What is their history? Where do the raw materials come from? How are they and the manufactured goods carried from one land to another? The story of transport and communication is in itself a thrilling romance. Don't look upon the things you handle merely as commodities. They have a history, just as the human race has a past. Who buy these things? Why? What sort of people are they? How do they spend their lives?

To read about these human, historical, geographical, and scientific aspects of your stock-in-trade is not only to find recreation; you will make your daily round more significant; you may give meaning to dull routine; you may see how, though your part might appear very small, it is very vital to the happiness of others.

If you are engaged in professional work – what other men have gone before you? How did they shape *their* lives? Can their experience teach you anything?

Lastly, there are your hobbies and recreations. They too have their wider aspects. Pursue them, and the mere pastime becomes more worth while, more valuable. Should your pleasure be listening to music, what of its history, of the lives of the composers and performers, of the poems and stories they have set to music, of the instruments upon which it is played? Should you collect stamps, who are all those men whose portraits are there in your album? Where are the countries whence the stamps came? What are they like? What of the story of the postal service? How is it operated? Is it chess, or bridge, there are books of problems and games. One could continue for ever.

Even a country walk can be made more beneficial, more fascinating by the use of books. Trees and flowers are just trees and flowers, birds just birds, churches just churches, unless you can distinguish one tree, one flower, from another, and know the peculiarities and particular charms of each, unless you know which bird it is that is making such delightful music, unless you can tell why this church is different from others, that this feature is unique, that one associated with some outstanding historical event.

If you could take your walks accompanied by a wise friend who, from an exceptional store of knowledge, could explain everything, you would certainly not refuse his company. Books can serve you in much the same way. There are pocket handbooks to help you to identify everything in field, hedgerow, pond or woodland – butterflies, insects, animals, fungi, ferns – everything. There are handy guide books telling you what to look for in every church or old building and why they are worth pausing to consider. At home in the evening, or during the winter months, the studies begun in the open air can be pursued in thousands of different books – and on no subjects have more pleasantly written, well illustrated, delightful volumes

been written than on nature study, local history, topo-
graphy, the manners and customs of the people, and all
those aspects of life encountered on your wanderings –
peaceful, happy books, too, most of them, offering a charm-
ing refuge from the troubles and difficulties of the daily
round.

We are left with purely recreational reading. If you have
developed the art of reading for interest you will have little
time for the other, but you will almost certainly have *some*.
One does not always want to be purposive or to read with a
motive. There are occasions when, maybe, it is a choice
between a siesta or a book. There is no harm in preferring
a book and no need to apologize if that book isn't Shakespeare. The golden rule in reading is always to choose the
most interesting book you are capable of enjoying at any
particular moment.

We are apt to make the mistake of regarding people as
either high-brow *or* low-brow, serious *or* frivolous, intellectual or *not*. Actually we are all a mixture of all these things,
and, according to our moods and our circumstances, each of
us will now be one and then the other. It doesn't do to take
life or ourselves too seriously. All work and no play make
Jack a dull boy. The man who can't enjoy a good joke probably won't really understand many of the more serious
aspects of life either. If he has not a sense of humour he is
not likely to have a sense of proportion. Life is just as funny
as it is sad, just as happy-go-lucky as it is deadly earnest. We
need relief and variety in all our pursuits. The great
dramatists know that, and nearly always go out of their
way to introduce comic relief into their tragedies.

So don't despise the lighter side of literature, but
remember that there are other books as well.

Read widely. One of the great advantages of reading is
that it enables you to learn about things which lie outside
your own personal experience. If you confine yourself to
one small set of subjects, to one type of book, you are
throwing away that advantage.

You should, if you would be happy and useful to the community, know *something* about the most important aspects of life – the world in which you live; its structure and surface features; the different countries and what they are like; what manner of men and women live in them; nature in all its phases; the how, why and wherefore of life; evolution; man and how he is made; how to keep healthy; how your mind works; how to develop your mental capabilities; your fellow-men and your relations with them; how you are governed and how you can play your part as an intelligent citizen; social diseases, war, crime and the like, and how to control them; education and its aims; the history of mankind; the important events of the past and their present-day significance; the lives and works of great men; art in its many forms and its value; the teachings of religion and philosophy.

This is a very sketchy outline – a mere skeleton map of knowledge.

You will, by wide reading, gradually pick up and piece together this foundation of essential information. By reading in a groove you won't. There are few more useless – and even dangerous – people than those who know a lot about just one thing and nothing about anything else. They have no sense of proportion; they cannot apply their specialized knowledge, because as soon as they try to do so they come up against *other* things they don't understand. Everything in this world is related to everything else – it may be very, very indirectly, but the influence is there. Everything we do, or even think, has some effect, sooner or later, upon other people; everything *they* do, everything that happens or exists, vaguely and indirectly or definitely and urgently affects *us*. Can we afford to remain totally ignorant of the many factors that are influencing our lives? We can't know *much*, but let what we *do* know be the most useful and varied. So, in your reading seek to acquire a background of general knowledge and *then* specialize in the subject that is most useful or interesting to you. In fact, even while you *are* specializing you should keep up your general reading.

There is another good reason for this advice. *Unless* you read widely you will not know what you miss. The most experienced, most adventurous literary explorers will always find some new enchantments waiting them. None of us can visit many of the thousand countries of the world of literature; we must scamper through all but perhaps one small province. If you had the time, the money and the health, would you be content to spend all your life in one place, be it Bethnal Green or Bedgellert? No. You would *travel*. Where books are concerned it costs no more to travel, to go abroad, than it does to stay at home. So see all you can.

Yet those of us who come into contact with book users know that most of them are singularly stay-at-home in their habits. They will tell you they are not interested in science, or history, or biography, or travel, or whatever it might be; and if you ask them if they have ever *tried* to read about these themes they reply 'Of *course* not', quite surprised at your question. It·is as though those who had never been to Wales (or Switzerland, or anywhere) told you that they hated the place. The same applies to novels. Most fiction readers have a few favourite authors whose works they have enjoyed. They will read everything and anything these may write, but you will have the greatest difficulty in persuading them to try other authors whose works will please them no less, and probably more. They won't experiment.

We cannot overlook the fact that it is difficult to choose enjoyable books. There are thousands each one of us *will* enjoy, but there are probably tens of thousands each one of us *won't* like. The reader is apt to think: 'I have so little time for reading that I must not waste it.' Exactly. But if you should select a book, from your library shall we say, and you find you don't like it – as you will do before you have gone far with it – you are under no compulsion to waste any more time upon it. Give it up and try another. There is no need to finish every book you start.

This may sound very dangerous advice – and it would be were you not sensible in your attitude towards books. Many a masterpiece which later you will cherish may, when you first approach it, seem dull and difficult. It may repel you. Its outlook may be so different from what you feel it should be; its ideas may be so new to you, that you are quite out of sympathy with them. Shall you – because of what has just been said – make no attempt to overcome this unfavourable first impression? The answer is 'No'.

There are two reasons why you won't like a book, why it will fail to interest or please you. On the one hand, it might have nothing to give you: no new ideas; no charm of style. You feel at once that it is an inferior book, that its attitude is false, or that you have already read it all before in other and better books. In other words, you don't like it because it is not good enough. Discard it without hesitation. On the other hand, however, you may sense that the fault is not so much with the book as with yourself, that you are a little prejudiced against its outlook, that you disagree, or you might be just a little too lazy to make the necessary effort to find out what it is all about. You might have the feeling that though you don't like it there is nevertheless 'something in it', something that it might be worth your while to discover. Such books present a different problem. Treat books as you would the men and women you meet in your daily life. Some are so obviously shallow, narrow minded and commonplace that you have no desire to cultivate their acquaintance; others you like instinctively; others you might find elusive, strange, 'different', but you feel that they have character. These arouse your interest; you want to know them better; and usually they improve on acquaintance, and from them you may learn much of value. So it is with books.

Conduct your experiments with discretion, however. When you decide to read about some fresh subject, choose the particular book with care, for if you should select an unsuitable one – either an inferior one or one intended for readers with more knowledge of the theme than you possess – it might do more to kill your interest than to stimulate it. Similarly, if you would try a new novelist, ascertain which is his best or his most appealing story or you might judge him by his most inferior and least typical book. Seek advice – from your librarian, or bookseller, or from the many printed guides to literature to be mentioned later.

When seeking advice about reading you may go to older friends, or you may turn to some of the books on 'literary taste and how to acquire it', or with some such title. Accept this advice with respect, but don't forget that you belong to the twentieth century. The present writer has just picked up such a 'guide' – published only a few years ago. In it the novice is recommended to read – as an *introduction* to literature – such books as Browne's RELIGIO MEDICI, Ruskin's FORS CLAVIGERA, Smith's WEALTH OF NATIONS, Berkeley's PRINCIPLES OF HUMAN KNOWLEDGE, Spencer's FIRST PRINCIPLES, and Taylor's HOLY LIVING.

You may often, unfortunately, be given advice like that, and it is dangerous. The books that writer mentions are great works, undoubtedly, and perhaps ten or twenty years hence you may enjoy them. Now they will only bore you or dishearten you. Your outlook is that of the post-war generation. You seek qualities and ideas closely related to your own difficult times. You lack the leisure to devote to the monumental tomes of the past. You want your information to be up to date, and in all fields of activity recent research has brought to light new information of vital importance.

This may sound rank blasphemy to some older readers, but our only concern here is that you should come to love books and be keen to relate literature to life – to your own life. And the classical works, and especially the classical books on history, science and the like, are not for you yet. The best approach to literature for you is found in the writings of your own generation, the books of men who face the same problems as you do, who share your environment. There are exceptions to every rule, and some books are timeless and belong to all ages alike. But there are not many of these.

Furthermore, read with discrimination.

You would all laugh at the story of the country yokel who said that as it was in print it must be true; but you may not appreciate the fact that 'print' *does* carry with it a certain suggestion of authority. Unless we are deliberately critical and alert it is very easy to accept without question whatever we read in books (even if we are more sceptical about newspapers). We say to ourselves, subconsciously: 'This man must know what he is talking about or he wouldn't write; neither would his books be published.' For this attitude there is some justification; quite a majority of informative books are undeniably accurate. You may recognize the author, by his qualifications or by the positions he holds, as one speaking with authority; you may know with certainty that if the publisher is one of repute (how little credit the average reader awards this partner in the production!), so far as fact is concerned, all the books he publishes are reliable, for no publisher of standing would publish any book unless it were by a recognized authority until he had first submitted the manuscript to one or more advisers thoroughly qualified to judge its accuracy.

Nevertheless, a great many of the topics dealt with in books are not entirely concerned with *facts*. ('What is truth?' asked Pilate.) To some extent they must embrace opinion. And no intelligent reader can afford to accept the opinion of any one man without some reservation, without, at least, realizing that it *is* opinion.

Therefore you must read with an open mind, prejudiced neither for nor against and, equally, not to be influenced unduly by persuasive, clever presentation. Whatever you read, unless it be mathematical tables, dates, or similar matter about which there can be no question, weigh the evidence, sift the facts, criticize the opinions to the utmost of your ability. Not only will you in this way be able to arrive at a better understanding of the truth; you will, by reading critically, exercise your own mind. And that is worth doing more than any mere assimilation of other people's ideas.

Remember that you yourself, because of your prejudices and ideals – and we all have both – may be an active obstacle to full understanding. Don't jump to the conclusion that because you disagree with a writer he must be wrong, or because he confirms your opinions that you must both be right. Read widely. Try always to judge the treatment of things about which you have little or no knowledge by comparing the handling of matters about which you are better informed.

Be on the look out for the superficial book; the book written by one with little real understanding of his subject, though, perhaps, with a flair for popular treatment, may be dangerous if a proper balance is sacrificed to a desire to emphasize the most interesting and spectacular aspects, or if it skates over the real difficulties.

Look out, also, for the work of propagandists. Read it by all means, but do so with open eyes.

Critical reading is much better than the stolid acceptance of whatever you may find in books. By bringing forward the ideas and knowledge we already possess and mixing them with the new material we are thus making the book part of our intellectual stock and assisting our memory.

CHAPTER THREE

WHAT BOOKS ARE THERE?

Now, however, we must be practical.

'I am told', you might say, 'that there are books on everything under the sun, and that I should read on this, that and the other topic just as the spirit moves me. But how am I to *get* the books I want? How, indeed, am I to know what books there are? I can't go into a bookshop and say that I want a book on "so-and-so", can I?'

In reply to the last part of the question one might ask: 'Why not?' The bookseller is in a better position than most to find out what books exist on any specific subject, and should be, and generally is, willing to go to whatever trouble is necessary to trace those which will best meet your needs. The same applies to the librarian. Neither expect you to give them the authors, titles, date and what-not of all the books you want. Many people would have to do without books if they did. Tell them exactly what you have in mind and they will make suitable recommendations. Nevertheless, you will want to learn for yourself something of the book world.

First of all, to get a general background, go to the best bookseller's shop in your town and glance systematically through the entire stock. Notice the range of subjects and the proportionate representation of the different main classes. Note in your mind the names of authors and the sort of books they write. Observe the publishers' names and see what kinds of books they publish and how well or how badly their output is produced. The reader is usually very ignorant regarding publishers and their work. Not one in a hundred could tell you the publisher of the book he is now reading (but let the publisher not be *too* despondent, for quite a few wouldn't even know the *author's* name!). This is a great mistake, because all publishers have their own special virtues, individual interests and strengths and weaknesses. Professional book-buyers pay considerable heed to this factor at times. Obviously we cannot describe here the merits and demerits of actual publishers, but book-buyers and book-users should study the matter.

This first visit will, if the shop is well stocked – and many alas are *not* – show the inquirer something of the immense variety – in price, appeal, get-up and subject – of the current output.

Make a regular habit of visiting bookshops wherever you happen to be. Have no hesitation about this, whether you have a purchase in mind or not. Usually you will find something you will *want* to buy before it is time to leave, but if you don't, or if you cannot then afford any purchase, the bookseller is not at all likely to object. On the contrary, he will welcome you as a potential customer, as one who appreciates and values books, as one who will probably influence others to buy them at some time or other, because you share a common interest with him. But of booksellers more later.

Next explore a few second-hand booksellers' premises – a much more adventurous and varied, if not sometimes so cleanly, undertaking. There are many admirably arranged, well-stocked, scrupulously dustless second-hand shops; there are others where all the despised and rejected volumes in existence seem to have been gathered together haphazard, piled on the floor or shelved near the ceiling for preference, and then sprinkled daily with the dust of ages. Nevertheless, the second-hand shop can exercise a strange fascination – and it can be a very necessary institution for the student, who will soon learn that many of the books he most needs are no longer obtainable new.

At the same time – all this, of course, assumes that you are not already a regular book-user – go to the nearest public library and apply for tickets for the lending department (see Chapter V). You will be allowed to go to the shelves and thus have access to several thousands of volumes. Spend as long as you can browsing and wandering from case to case. Go into the Reference Department of the same institution and examine as much of the stock as you may. Your knowledge of books will be increasing daily.

Whether you are new to libraries or not – and the same applies to bookshops – avoid getting into the habit of going straight to one bookcase or shelf embracing your pet subject. You will miss much that way. Try to explore the whole stock gradually. Don't even be content when you have been right round once. Start again. The stock on the shelves is constantly changing.

So much for a general view. Now let us see how you may find out about those books you want yourself.

The world of books is so vast that if we are to find our way about we must take full advantage of the many signposts, maps, guide books and gazetteers of literature. But that doesn't make our task a simple one. On the contrary there are so many signposts, maps, etc., that we must first learn to find our way about *them*. So let us proceed systematically: firstly, what about the books that have just been published and those which are soon to be published? Secondly, how can we get information about less recent books? Thirdly, what books are there about different subjects?

(*a*) FOR INFORMATION REGARDING NEW PUBLICATIONS:

1. Read the reviews and notices of books given in various periodicals.

Only one paper (*The Times Literary Supplement*, weekly, threepence) covers the whole field at all thoroughly. Few publications, be they weighty tomes on Hittite inscriptions, cricket almanacks, or novels, are missed, and the reviewing is concise and authoritative. The longer reviews are very readable, so if you are really interested in books you are advised to see the *T.L.S.*, as it is popularly called, regularly.

Literary works and books of general interest on social, historical and similar topics are to some extent covered by a number of weekly reviews, such as *The New Statesman and Nation, The Spectator, Time and Tide*, and others. Much the same field is covered by certain daily papers, such as the *Daily Telegraph* and the *News Chronicle*, while, for general books probably the best guides (after the *T.L.S.*) are those splendid weeklies, the *Sunday Times* and the *Observer*. All these periodicals, however, only consider a small selection chosen because of their wide appeal, so don't expect to find everything mentioned in them. *John o'London's Weekly* is an excellent and very readable periodical almost entirely concerned with books and readers.

2. For reviews of more specialized books one must consult the various professional, technical, trade and class papers, most of which review new publications of special interest to their readers. (For example, books on art in *The Studio*, on science in *Nature*, on engineering in *The Engineer*, and so on.) Some periodicals do this well, but many don't. Find out which is the best periodical for your subject. Classified lists of periodicals will be found in *Mitchell's Newspaper Press Directory*, *Willing's Press Guide*, and *Black's Writers' and Artists' Year Book*. These may be seen at any library. The periodicals themselves may also be available in the reading-rooms at your library.

3. Every publisher will send you, on request, copies of his catalogues and lists of announcements. Some firms also issue interesting and well-produced 'house organs', consisting of reviews of and extracts from their publications, which are sent freely on request. The best of these are small literary magazines well worth reading for their own sake.

Some publishers use a postcard form (which you will find inserted in their books), on which you can mark the subjects about which you particularly desire information, but if you are wise you will also get their general announcements. They will also send you prospectuses of their books – leaflets giving a brief description with, perhaps, a specimen page and illustration.

The war has, of course, reduced the amount of information publishers have been able to circulate and, indeed, the demand for books in short supply has often been such that little publicity was needed. Such conditions are, however, only temporary.

4. Nevertheless readers should keep a watch on advertisements and other announcements of 'forthcoming' books. These appear in the periodicals already mentioned as including 'reviews' and also in the book-trade periodicals, *The Bookseller* and *The Publishers' Circular* (to be seen at most bookshops and libraries – and about which more will be said later). To-day the only way one can be sure of buying some books is to order them before publication – not always a satisfactory proposition unless the buyer knows all he can about the characteristics and qualities of the authors and publishers concerned – especially the latter.

5. In this and many other ways the good bookseller can be the book-buyer's best friend. Tell your bookseller about your own interests and requirements. He can often advise both what to buy and what *not* to buy.

6. He will also provide you regularly with one or other of those excellent monthly lists of new books – Whitaker's *Current Literature* and Simpkin, Marshall's *Books of the Month*. In both, the books are arranged in main subject classes with author indexes; they also include reviews and interesting articles on books.

Complete lists of new publications appear every week in *The Bookseller* and *The Publisher's Circular*, with a monthly cumulation in the issue for the last week of each month.

The British Council and the National Book League are jointly responsible for *British Book News*, a monthly descriptive list of important and representative publications. The annotations are particularly full – as the list is intended for circulation to book-users and booksellers throughout the world. At present *B.B.N.* is not obtainable in Great Britain, owing to paper restrictions.

7. Wireless book talks are of value, though at present they embrace such a small part of the total output of books, and that part consists mostly of books of which all who read reviews will be well aware already, that the talks are not so

useful as they might be. It would be very valuable if from time to time – even once every month or two – specialists could draw attention to recent publications in their own fields, such as new books on science, new plays, new gardening books, new children's books, and so on. In passing it should be said that at present children's books are not at all adequately reviewed in the daily Press, but there is one periodical entirely devoted to them — the quarterly *Junior Book Shelf* — and much information and evaluation appears in *John o' London's Weekly*.

(*b*) FOR INFORMATION ABOUT LESS RECENT PUBLICATIONS: Often we want to know who published a book, who wrote one of which we know only the title, when it was published, at what price, and other such information.

8. There are two annual lists of British publications (to be seen at most libraries and booksellers) –

WHITAKER'S CUMULATIVE BOOK LIST and THE ENGLISH CATALOGUE.

The former is based on the weekly and monthly lists in *The Bookseller* and in Whitaker's *Current Literature*. Entries are arranged under main subjects, with an author and title index; there are quarterly cumulations and a yearly volume; a five-year cumulation for the years 1939-43 has been published.

The English Catalogue gives an alphabetical list of authors and titles, together with a directory of publishers and particulars of Government publications and of the publications of learned and scientific societies. At the time of writing the latest volume available was that for 1943. Earlier volumes cover British publications since 1801.

9. For books still 'in print' in 1938 consult WHITAKER'S REFERENCE CATALOGUE OF CURRENT LITERATURE which contains over half a million author, title and subject entries.

10. There is a similar American publication to be consulted at many public libraries – H. W. WILSON'S CUMULATIVE BOOK INDEX, published monthly, with quarterly, annual and five-year cumulations. It lists not only Ameri-

can publications but also books in the English language published in all countries since 1929, with entries under authors, titles, subjects, etc. For American books 'in print' in 1928 see THE UNITED STATES CATALOG, the forerunner of *The Cumulative Book Index*.

11. The same American firm has given the book-using world several other important reference works, some of which will be noted later. Here we would refer to a somewhat unusual work for which there is no British counterpart: THE BOOK REVIEW DIGEST, issued monthly, with six-monthly, annual and five-yearly cumulations. This does not merely list some 4000 important books, mostly American, each year; it gives summaries of the leading reviews showing whether they are favourable or otherwise.

12. The British BEST BOOKS OF THE YEAR, published annually by *The Librarian*, is a select classified list.

See also the A.S.L.I.B. BOOK LIST, 'quarterly recommendations of recently-published scientific and technical books', an authoritative publication issued by the Association of Special Libraries and Information Bureaux.

(c) FOR GUIDANCE REGARDING BOOKS ON PARTICULAR SUBJECTS:

13. The outstanding subject list is the BRITISH MUSEUM'S SUBJECT INDEX OF MODERN BOOKS.

The first volumes embraced books published between 1881 and 1900, but supplementary volumes are brought out every five years. Brief entries are given under subject headings, and, as the British Museum adds nearly every British publication and most foreign ones of importance, it will be realized that this is a very valuable guide.

A complementary, non-official, work is R. A. PEDDIE'S SUBJECT INDEX OF BOOKS PUBLISHED BEFORE 1880, 3 series, 1933-39.

Of almost equal value is the SUBJECT INDEX OF THE LONDON LIBRARY, 1909, and two supplements covering books added to this great circulating library between 1909 and 1938.

14. The above aim at 'completeness' rather than 'selection'. There are two extensive general select lists of books arranged in classified order and giving brief information about the scope, price, date, etc. of each. Both are unfortunately somewhat out of date but are still valuable for older material. They are SONNENSCHEIN'S BEST BOOKS, 3rd edn., 5 vols., 1910-31, with a sixth, index, volume published in 1935, and NELSON'S STANDARD BOOKS, 4 vols., 1912-15.

A much smaller work, also out of date but still useful, is W. FORBES GRAY'S BOOKS THAT COUNT, 1923.

15. Two good descriptive basic lists of books suitable for medium-sized (American) libraries are THE AMERICAN LIBRARY ASSOCIATION CATALOG, 1926, an annotated list of 10,000 items, with supplements for 1926-31 and 1932-36, and H. W. WILSON'S STANDARD CATALOG FOR PUBLIC LIBRARIES, 1940, a list of 12,000 books, with annual supplements.

16. Two useful single volume guides are BESSIE GRAHAM'S BOOKMAN'S MANUAL, 5th edn., 1941, an American handbook for booksellers and book-users, with 43 chapters devoted to literature of different types and on various subjects, and the British J. M. ROBERTSON'S COURSES OF STUDY, 3rd edn., 1932.

THE LIBRARY ASSOCIATION'S BOOKS TO READ, 1930, with a supplement, 1931, is intended as a guide for adolescent readers, but actually goes further, describing an excellent basic selection for the general reader, particularly the newcomer to books.

The above-mentioned works cover the whole range of knowledge, but there are also a great many lists – they are called 'bibliographies ' – each devoted to a particular subject. We shall refer to these again; first we would mention a few of these special bibliographies in three fields of very general importance – English literature, fiction, and reference books.

17. The advanced student of English literature is well

served by THE CAMBRIDGE BIBLIOGRAPHY OF ENGLISH
LITERATURE, 4 vols., 1941, which aims at recording every
written book from the earliest times to 1900, which can be
included under the head of English literature, together with
biographical and critical literature about the most important
writers.

The beginner, however, will welcome F. SEYMOUR SMITH'S
AN ENGLISH LIBRARY, 1943 (4th edition 1946), an annotated
list of 1300 classics, published by the National Book League.
The same author is preparing a similar work dealing with
living authors. Meanwhile, for recent writers see F. B.
MILLETT'S CONTEMPORARY BRITISH LITERATURE, 3rd ed.,
1935, a critical survey with 232 author bibliographies, and
a similar work by the same author, CONTEMPORARY
AMERICAN AUTHORS.

Your public library may also have three interesting
American publications by S. J. KUNITZ and H. HAYCROFT
entitled TWENTIETH CENTURY AUTHORS, BRITISH AUTHORS
OF THE 19TH CENTURY and AMERICAN AUTHORS, 1600-
1900. Each volume embraces brief biographies of over a
thousand authors with lists of their books and many
portraits.

SIR PAUL HARVEY'S OXFORD COMPANION TO ENGLISH
LITERATURE, 1947, is a comprehensive dictionary of
authors, books, characters, allusions, etc.

The same author's OXFORD COMPANION TO CLASSICAL
LITERATURE, 1937, embraces information which the ordinary reader, not only of the literature of Greece and Rome
but also of that large proportion of modern European literature which teems with classical allusions, may find useful.

See also the BIOGRAPHICAL DICTIONARY OF ENGLISH
LITERATURE and BIOGRAPHICAL DICTIONARY OF FOREIGN
LITERATURE, both in Everyman's Library. Incidentally
one whole volume in this famous library is a READER'S
GUIDE TO EVERYMAN'S LIBRARY, and the scope of the series
is so extensive that the guide is a useful conspectus of basic
literature. Students will also find the full descriptive lists

of this and such other series as the World's Classics of much interest.

18. Secondly, as most of you read novels – and if you don't you should – here are some useful guides to standard and current fiction.

The most important is E. A. BAKER and JAMES PACKMAN'S GUIDE TO THE BEST FICTION, 1932, a list of noteworthy English and American novels and translations from foreign languages with a most valuable subject index. If you are interested in historical novels see E. A. BAKER'S GUIDE TO HISTORICAL FICTION, 1914. Much of the material is incorporated in the *Guide*, but as here the arrangement is by country and period it is not really replaced.

See also a similar work, JONATHAN NIELD'S GUIDE TO THE BEST HISTORICAL NOVELS AND TALES, 1929.

THE FICTION CATALOG, 1941, an American publication by the H. W. Wilson Co., describes 5500 typical novels. Annual supplements are published.

It often happens that an author – and his readers – are so fascinated by the characters of a novel that their later experiences are embodied in one or even several later stories, as for example in the famous series by Alexander Dumas, the 'Forsyte Saga' of Galsworthy and the 'Whiteoaks' books of Mazo De La Roche. You will be reminded of such series and enabled to read them in the right order if you consult: T. ALDRED'S SEQUEL STORIES, ENGLISH AND AMERICAN, 2nd ed., by W. H. Parker, 1928. A new edition is in preparation.

19. There are three important guides to *reference books* – the first two published by the American Library Association, the third by our own Library Association:

I. G. MUDGE'S GUIDE TO REFERENCE BOOKS, 5th ed., 1929, with four supplements bringing it up to 1946;

H. S. HIRSHBERG'S SUBJECT GUIDE TO REFERENCE BOOKS, 1942; and

JOHN MINTO'S REFERENCE BOOKS, 1929, with a supplement published in 1931.

May we also mention LIBRARY STOCK AND ASSISTANCE TO READERS, 1936, by the author of this book in collaboration with his brother, E. R. McColvin? Intended primarily as a textbook for library assistants, it describes outstanding reference books of all kinds, lists typical books on a wide variety of subjects and gives a series of exercises in fact finding and inquiry methods. If you are tired of reading detective stories and would do some detective work on your own you will find those exercises an intriguing pastime.

20. All four works just mentioned describe many bibliographies devoted to special subjects of all kinds – engineering, science, history, art and a thousand more. Every reader who has a specialized interest should make a point of ascertaining what 'special' bibliographies exist. Not only will these bibliographies save hours of research and disappointment – they will open doors to unsuspected wealth.

Further sources of information about bibliographies are mentioned in the companion volume to this work – HOW TO FIND OUT.

In addition to the longer bibliographies numerous short book-lists are found in many treatises, textbooks and works of reference. For example, at the end of most of the articles in encyclopaedias there are lists of useful books in which the matter can be pursued further. Similar lists are even to be found in articles in scientific, technical and learned periodicals.

21. Several public libraries issue from time to time carefully selected short book-lists devoted to special subjects and recent publications. Ask if your own library publishes any. Even if it doesn't it may possess examples from other libraries – such as Bristol, Sheffield or Luton, to name but three places which do excellent work in this field.

Other libraries – for example, Norwich, Nottingham and Portsmouth – either in addition to or instead of these subject lists publish monthly or quarterly 'bulletins' describing recent additions and outlining the library's activities and facilities. *The Manchester Review*, published quarterly by the

Manchester Public Libraries, is a splendid example. One of the earliest still appearing is the Croydon *Reader's Index*.

THE READERS' GUIDES, issued by the County Libraries Section of the Library Association just before and early in the war, were an excellent effort in co-operation. Over thirty of the Guides, each of about 20 pages, have appeared dealing, among other subjects, with handicrafts, modern poetry, psychology, child study and mothercraft, physical fitness, civics, astronomy, music, the history of painting, gardening, house and home, and rural life. The information given includes date, publisher and price, and all the books listed are of appeal to the ordinary reader and are readily obtainable from most libraries.

22. The most extensive series of book lists is, however, that published by the NATIONAL BOOK LEAGUE. These lists, all compiled by experts and authoritative bodies, range from a single sheet to, in one case, 56 pages. This last – on British Civilization and Institutions – was edited by L. R. McColvin and J. Revie, who had the help of dozens of eminent specialists. Others among the over two hundred varied lists now issued — the compilers are noted in parentheses — deal with Aeronautical Engineering (Royal Aeronautical Society), Anthropology (Royal Anthropological Institute), Architecture (Royal Institute of British Architects), The British Commonwealth (Royal Empire Society), Building Construction (Building Research Station), Christianity and Social Problems (Industrial Christian Fellowship), Economics and Public Finance (B. M. Headicar), Food (King's College of Household and Social Science), Health (Society of Medical Officers of Health), History (A. S. Turberville), Maps (Royal Geographical Society), Medicine and Surgery (British Medical Association), Nursing (Royal College of Nursing), and Reference Books (W. A. Munford). New editions are brought out at frequent intervals.

You may see these lists at your public library or booksellers, but if you are wise you will join the National Book

League and have them sent to you free of charge as they appear. This, however, is only one of the benefits you will secure.

The National Book League is a society uniting all those who are interested in books – the authors, the publishers, the printers and binders, booksellers, librarians, educationists and readers. The importance of such an organization to a modern society can scarcely be exaggerated. Its activities are many sided. It provides members with information and guidance on all aspects of book-use by means, for example, of the book-lists already mentioned, its monthly *News Sheet*, its Information Bureau and its comprehensive Library. It brings together book-loving people at its meetings and its branches, its lectures and exhibitions; its new headquarters in Albemarle Street has become a literary rendezvous. It seeks in many ways to promote the wider and more fruitful utilization of books in schools, technical and training colleges, and the like. It organizes 'Book Weeks' – notably for children. It maintains valuable contacts with such other agencies as the Arts Council, the British Drama League, the B.B.C., the British Council and the Library Association. Above all it enables the book-world to speak as a united whole. This has never been possible before – and it has never been so necessary. In the great task of building a brave new world books have an essential part to play but, with so many other matters making urgent claims upon the attention of the public and the government and upon the national resources of material and labour, the needs of the book-user are in danger of being overlooked and denied their place in the national economy unless a powerful and independent organization, like the N.B.L., is able and ready to stress their proper importance.

We will, however, say no more here. Any interested reader of this book – and every reader *should* be interested – can obtain full particulars of the League by writing to 7 Albemarle Street, London, W.1.

CHAPTER FOUR

ON BUYING BOOKS

Now you know what books there are, the next question is, 'How may I obtain them?'

Books, like everything else, one may beg, buy, borrow or steal. There is, however, the important difference between books and most other things, that the last two methods predominate. Of all the things men and women use, books are the most frequently borrowed and, if failure to return be theft, the most often stolen.

There is, however, a special reason why books are so often borrowed. On the one hand, many may read the same copy of a book and, if they treat it properly, the last can enjoy it as much as the first. On the other hand, there are very many books that none of us want to read twice. So far as a large proportion of books are concerned it would be sheer waste not to lend and borrow them. More than that – in one way and another, for study, work and recreation, we may use so many books that, had we to purchase all of them we should need to be very wealthy men. Nevertheless, we *must* buy some books, even though our purses are slender – *must* because we need to refer to them constantly, or because we love them so much that we would not be separated from them. No matter how highly developed and efficient commercial and public institutions for lending books may become, we *all* need our own home libraries. We must buy and beg as well as borrow, and the wise reader will intelligently combine the three methods to his own best advantage.

Each must answer the question 'to buy or not to buy' according to his own means and conscience. There are thousands of students in the country for whom the purchase of even a few books might mean hardship. They are the exception, however, and though the writer would not advocate the purchase of the hundreds of volumes each of you will want to read or consult, to borrow too much and to buy too little is a bad thing – bad both for the reader and for the publishers and booksellers upon whom you depend for the supply of books.

It is easy to forget that publishing and bookselling are business concerns and if too many people, able to buy, are content to borrow, the time will come when it won't be a paying proposition to publish and sell certain types of book at all, if, indeed, that time is not here already.

Speaking generally, everyone who can should (for his own sake) purchase his own copies of:

(a) His favourite works of literature, both the master-pieces and those, perhaps lesser, books, which have a personal association and appeal. These he may want to read – or perhaps lend to friends – at any time.

(b) A small collection of reference books – dictionaries, a small encyclopaedia, atlases, almanacs, etc. It is essential to have such books in every house where intelligent folk have to live.

(c) Textbooks, standard treatises and other books relating to his studies or hobbies and which he will require for several months on end, or to which he will have frequent occasion to refer. These are books which he needs for a longer time than he could reasonably borrow them for from any library. They are in the nature of being special reference works on his subject. If he relies on being able to re-borrow them from a library whenever he requires them he is bound soon to be disappointed and maybe seriously inconvenienced by finding them in the hands of other readers.

(d) Especially if there are children in the household – a few comprehensive illustrated books on themes of general interest, such as the world and its people, history, science and the like. Children can do much to educate themselves, and to find amusement and occupation, if there are plenty of suitable books handy for rainy days.

(e) A few beautiful books, representative of good production, books that can be treasured and treated with respect. *All* books should be, of course, but here one thinks of those which *demand* a respect seldom awarded an 'ordinary' volume. We collect beautiful pictures and china and so on to make our homes more pleasant, so why not a few beautiful books?

(f) Perhaps a little specialist collection. It will help to maintain enthusiasm for a topic if books dealing with its varied phases are purchased from time to time. Such severely limited little libraries can often, if well selected, be of considerable value, and at the worst they are an excuse for keeping in touch with book-production and bookshops.

Bookshops – *new* bookshops, that is – vary considerably, from those in the larger cities and a few in some of the smaller towns, too, that carry a large stock from which most of your normal requirements can be produced on demand, to those with a few shelves of cheap editions of novels hidden behind greeting cards and pie frills. Even the smallest, however, *can and will get you any obtainable volume.*

No tradesman has a more difficult stock to handle than a bookseller, and none has to take more trouble to satisfy those who, relatively, may spend very small sums. It is easy to grumble about the bookseller and his deficiencies; but ask any other tradesman how he would like to stock articles for which only one in a thousand of his customers might ask and which none of the others would have at any price, how he would like to attempt to make a selection of the greatest appeal to the generality of his customers when he knew all the time that the great majority would have highly individual and specialized tastes. That is the bookseller's position. Of the thousands of books published in a year how many can he be *certain* to sell in, say, a smallish town? Very few. All the rest are speculative. And as he cannot afford to speculate too much he cannot offer the selection he would wish.

But – as beforesaid – he can *get* anything – anything that is 'in print'. If he also deals in second-hand books he can often get those that aren't also (but see later).

Your bookseller, indeed, can be very useful.

You may want a book on a certain subject to suit your special needs, and he will help to discover one for you. He may probably know from his long experience *just* the one you require. Many booksellers have a remarkable know-ledge of books and memories that arouse our envy. And unless you are unlucky in your bookseller you will never find him suggesting an expensive book just because it *is* expensive, if it isn't the best for your purpose. This sounds very idealistic, but, if you think, you will find that in this respect the good bookseller is no more altruistic than the good grocer or butcher or any tradesman who hopes to serve you for many years to come. So do not hesitate to ask his advice.

In this connection it should be said that often you can use your public library to help you to select books for purchase. Say you wish to buy a history of France (or whatever it might be). Go to the public library, ask to see the various histories of France; among them you *may* find one to suit you.

To return to the new bookseller: He can trace the correct titles of books by a given author, or the author of a book with a given title, he can tell you the price and publisher, he can give you the date of publication – all useful informa-tion. Generally he has a flair, the result of long practice in satisfying vague customers, for tracing books even though the data you give him may be incomplete or misleading.

Sometimes, but only sometimes, he can get you books on approval so that you can see whether it is worth your pur-chasing them. But do not expect this, or feel that it is a normal privilege and be annoyed if it cannot be granted you. Many, indeed most, publishers will *not* send books to the bookseller on sale or return, as the system involves cer-tain complications and expenses, may lead to damaged stock and is liable to be abused. Furthermore, if your bookseller *does* get a volume on approval for you and you do *not* purchase it, you should be prepared, though you might not be asked, to pay the cost of postage.

Your bookseller will keep you informed of books on any subject and will send you any catalogues and prospectuses you want.

Nearly all new publications are sold at a *net* price, below which the bookseller *must* not sell them. So don't expect any discount. It cannot be given you.

A few words about the price of books: One can pay anything from a few pence to several pounds for a single volume, and every reader can therefore buy according to his purse. Thousands of interesting and well-produced books may be purchased for the price of a seat at the cinema or a small box of cigarettes, and if only readers appreciated the lasting pleasure of well chosen books they would regard them as by far the better investment for their money.

It is often said that books are too dear. You may sometimes also wonder why it is that two books of just the same length, with similar illustrations, equally well printed and bound, may differ considerably in price. One might be half-a-crown, the other seven-and-six; one five shillings, the other fifteen. The explanation is simple. The more copies a publisher can sell the cheaper they can be. This is true of most manufactured articles, but it is especially the case with books. The heaviest items of expense – for setting the type, making the blocks for the illustrations, designing the cover and jacket and several other costs – are the same whether three hundred or thirty thousand copies are sold. This cost can be spread over the whole *if* the publisher knows at the outset how many he is likely to sell. The publisher knows with certainty that many books will *not* sell in large numbers; these he must price at a higher figure, or he will lose heavily. Of many others, especially novels, he is very doubtful. He *might* sell a goodly number or he might not. It depends upon public taste, which is fickle. In such cases he has to price the publication at a customary average, and out of fairness to those who buy at that price he must maintain it for a reasonable time, after which he issues a 'Cheap Edition' – i.e. sells the book, possibly in a cheaper get-up, at a lower price, which he now knows will nevertheless repay him, as he will sell many copies. Because of war-time shortages of materials 'cheap editions' have, of course, become the exception rather than the rule but they will surely return when conditions improve.

There are, of course, other factors to be considered, but the point here is that publishers as a whole want books to be as cheap as they can possibly make them. Prices can only come down when you and all other readers buy as many books as you need and can afford.

The second-hand bookseller covers an even wider field, and, again, his specialized knowledge is most valuable to the book-user. When you need a special book which is no longer in print and if, as is probable, your local bookseller has no copy in stock, you may do one of two things:

(a) Send postcards to a number of likely firms asking them to 'report' if they have the work, when, if more than one copy is reported, you can compare prices and condition.

Or (b) you can ask your usual second-hand bookseller to do his best to obtain one at a fair price. He will probably advertise in one of the trade papers, such as *The Clique* or *The Publisher's Circular*. These are regularly scanned by hundreds of dealers throughout the country, and so, if copies are on the market, you will probably secure one by this means. If the book is not an expensive one he may charge you a few pence for advertising.

When asking for reports (or advertising) be sure to stipulate the particular *edition* you require (it may be the first or the latest or any other). This will save a lot of misunderstanding.

Most second-hand booksellers issue from time to time printed catalogues which it will interest you to receive. Send a postcard to dealers requesting them, and they will be sent to you as published. Once they were free of charge. During the war regulations concerning the free distribution of advertisements compelled booksellers to make a nominal charge for their lists – but it was only a temporary measure. Glancing through them one might notice hitherto unknown books of interest; the prices will be useful as a guide to future purchases. Some of these catalogues, such as those of Maggs, Edwards, Sotheran, Quaritch, Ellis and other large firms, are often detailed and sometimes illustrated surveys of special fields of literature and are well worth receiving and keeping for reference.

A list of booksellers, giving their specialities, will be found in *Booksellers Handbook* and *Clegg's International Directory of Booksellers*, while many advertise in *The Times Literary Supplement* and other papers.

Note that if you *particularly* want a book listed in any catalogue it is often worth sending a telegram ordering it, as other readers might be equally keen to secure it, and post will be too slow.

The novice will find it difficult to tell the proper price to pay for second-hand books (or to receive if he sells). Generally it is wisest, unless comparative and competitive prices are available, to rely upon a regular dealer one can trust. Where 'rare' books – first editions and the like – are concerned only long experience and expert knowledge can help. Often the reader will want books not for their rarity but for their own sake. Especially since the war many most useful books are out of print, and he will sometimes find that prices, if he would buy, are high. There are, to give two examples, certain musical biographies and one or two books on numismatics, which students still require; the second-hand price is much more than the original price because the demand exceeds the supply. If you are in doubt consult your public librarian, who will often be able to advise you.

All old books, however, are not valuable. If you come into possession of any venerable tomes, do not be disappointed if they are of little worth. *Most* old books are quite valueless.

Two useful reference books are *Book Auction Records* and *Book Prices Current* – annual publications which you may see at most libraries, and which record the sales of books at public auctions. Those sold in lots are not included, neither are those which only fetch trivial sums. Remember, however, that these are *auction* prices. If you want to buy from a dealer you will have to pay somewhat more, and if you want to sell you may be offered much less.

Another useful work, though limited in scope, is ENGLISH BOOKS, 1475-1900, by C. J. SAWYER and F. J. HARVEY DARTON, in two volumes.

This is an appropriate place to deal with book-collecting for its own sake as distinct from gathering together books because you want to use and read them. Until recently the collection of first editions was almost a craze, hundreds of books being even specially published in limited editions for collectors. The writer must record his opinion that collecting for rarity's sake has little to do with the genuine use of books. It may be a lucrative pursuit for the expert; it is also one at which the uninitiated can waste much time and money. In the long run the reader who buys books because he loves them, who collects an author because he enjoys his work, will, if his literary judgment is sound, possess a more valuable collection. *And*, if he should back the wrong horse financially, he will at least have bought pleasure and inspiration. For most who would collect more than the ordinary home library, specialization is the most interesting and useful plan.

A few words on certain classes of book you will encounter:

Remainders. Publishers' remainders are new copies of books sold at a price which is generally considerably below that at which they were originally published. They should be purchased with care. They are copies which could not be sold at the full price because the publishers had overestimated the demand. It does not by any means follow that they are inferior books; sometimes they are, but you may at times secure real bargains. It is very difficult to judge the right number to print. A book might, indeed, be very popular, but by the time an additional supply had been bound and made available the demand may have dropped, for popularity is very changeable. Again, many excellent publications for some reason or other do not find their market – they might come out before public interest in their theme is aroused or just after it has abated, they might be over-shadowed by more popular or cheaper competitors, they might be badly marketed, for *all* publishers are not perfect business men. In such case your remainder is probably worth while. On the other hand, lots of books are so inferior that they should never have been printed, and then the publisher seeks to recover part of his loss by disposing of the unwanted stock by remaindering it for whatever it will fetch. So you will be well advised to examine remainders carefully – though examine them by all means. There have not, of course, been many 'remainders' on the market since war broke out because, on the one hand, reputable publishers have been unable even to produce enough of the books they knew they could sell at normal prices, and, on the other, because the book shortage has caused even bad books to sell. Incidentally, far too many bad books *have* appeared in recent years – a double tragedy because they have used material and labour that could have been better employed.

Ex-Library Copies. The commercial circulating libraries dispose of surplus copies of the books they have lent from the libraries as soon as these have ceased to be in demand. They cannot sell them – under the agreement between the publishers and the libraries – until six months after publication. Often they are offered at attractive prices and are in good condition. It is difficult to advise. Having the welfare of the book trade at heart – as all constant book-users must have – the writer would always rather see a new copy purchased than an ex-library one, but he also knows that all readers have little to spend on books and so he is loathe to discourage them from adding in this way to their personal collections. Moreover, if the libraries could not sell their surplus stock they would not be able to purchase so many copies from the publishers in the first instance – and there is no doubt that the purchases of the circulating libraries alone make the publication of numerous novels and popular works of non-fiction possible at all.

So by all means buy ex-library books if you want them and cannot afford to buy them new. But never buy any book just because it is cheap.

Book Tokens were introduced a few years before the war with the very sensible idea that when you want to make a friend a present it is better to enable him to buy something he really wants than to send him something *you* think, perhaps quite wrongly, he *might* like – or which he may already possess. The scheme has been a great success and so it needs no advocacy here except to note one virtue which may be overlooked. Don't limit your book token gifts to friends who already buy books; send them also to those who don't. Thus you will introduce them to the joys of book buying and book possession.

CHAPTER FIVE

LIBRARIES

SOME publishers and booksellers regard libraries, of all kinds, as their enemies; they think that they prevent the sale of books which the public *would* buy were they not able to borrow them. A little impartial consideration, however, will show how false this attitude really is. In the first place, as we have already seen, there are many books which no one wants sufficiently to go to the expense of *buying* them. They will serve only for a few hours recreation. By combining together through some organization to share these books, readers actually make it possible for publishers to sell books for which they would otherwise have no market whatever; they sell them to the libraries instead of to individuals. Again, hardly any of us could afford to buy *many* books. If we could not borrow them it is probable that we should never acquire the book habit at all, for we should never appreciate the importance of book-use unless we made it part of our everyday life. Thirdly, there are thousands of books which, because of their rarity, or because they are out of print, or for many other reasons, we *cannot* obtain except at libraries. Most important of all, booksellers who object to libraries should realize their share in promoting that higher standard of education which alone can lead to the appreciation of good books. The tremendous increase in the output of books during the last sixty years may be due partly to compulsory education, but it is no less the result of the spread of library services.

It is also certain that those who borrow most are often those who buy most. Those who are content with the lighter literature they can obtain from circulating libraries are, moreover, not such as would buy anything except the cheapest and least valuable books were they unable to borrow at all.

There are many different kinds of libraries, each serving the varying needs of different sections of the community.

First of all there are the *Circulating* or *Subscription* Libraries – such as Boots, W. H. Smith's, The Times Book Club, etc. – and their lesser brethren, the shops whence, for twopence or threepence a week, novels may be borrowed 'without subscription or deposit'. These shops and the branches of the larger organizations are to be found in every town and village in the country.

Undoubtedly they play an important part in the supply of the more popular literature of the day, and their activities and facilities must be too well known to call for any description here. It should be noted that their range is somewhat limited – to fiction and 'general' literature (that is to say, biography, travel, history and the like, written to appeal to the average non-expert reader). Technical, scientific and specialist books are, as a rule, excluded. Neither – an even more important point – do they provide older and standard books, confining their activity to circulating the more recent publications. For the former the reader must have recourse to the public and specialist collections.

Roughly speaking, you should be able to obtain from the circulating libraries all books reviewed in the daily Press and, with a few exceptions, in the *Sunday Times* and *Observer* – naturally, since both cater for the generality of non-specialist readers.

Subscription rates are very low – some, in the trade, would say *too* low – and the best libraries give a remarkably good service. There are, in the main, three types of subscription – a guaranteed subscription for which the libraries undertake to provide on demand any book for which you ask (excepting technical, specialist and other specified types); a second grade, in which you may apply for books to be reserved for and issued to you at the earliest opportunity; and an ordinary subscription on which you must mak 2 whatever selection is possible from the stock available at the time, and for which, sometimes, newer books are not provided.

Whatever type of subscription yours may be, make it your business to find out exactly what you are entitled to have and see that you get it (and don't expect any more). We would undoubtedly recommend the 'guaranteed' or 'on demand' subscription; if you use it to the full you will be securing a remarkably cheap book service. For less than fivepence a volume you may, with one firm, have two books a week on this basis, books of your choice just when you want them.

For those who can afford it, the best plan for anyone who reads widely and reads a lot, is to have a guaranteed subscription on which to obtain all the new books he definitely wants to read there and then, and to use the public library for general purposes and for all the books (specialist and older) which he cannot get from the circulating libraries. Such a reader should be able to secure exactly what he wants when he wants it.

We revert, however, to the injunction, 'See that you get the full service for your subscription', and we do so not because we are Shylocks after our pounds of flesh. Neither are we suggesting that any good circulating library will try to evade its responsibilities. If yours did not fulfil its contract you would have the obvious remedy of transferring to another which would.

The point has, however, much wider implications. By insisting on having every book you want you are definitely helping publishers and other readers. Let us give a concrete example. A biography of XYZ is published. You read reviews, or see advertisements, and decide that it would interest you. You ask for it at your circulating library; if you are half-hearted you might not get it, but if you insist you will. How does that matter? Because you are one of perhaps a thousand other subscribers similarly interested in the life of XYZ. If you are *all* lukewarm very few copies of that book may be purchased by the libraries, and so when at some future time the same publisher is considering the manuscript of a similar book he will probably decide not to publish it. On the other hand, if all of you had exercised your right to read the book the resulting sale would have encouraged the publisher to give you a second one you would enjoy no less.

In other words, in a general way it is difficult for the reader to play his part in dictating what shall and what shall not be published. Here is one opportunity to show both publishers and libraries what you like. When readers *buy* their books direct from their booksellers the sales are, of course, a fairly clear indication to the publisher, but when books are borrowed from libraries sales mean little unless all the subscribers are asking for whatever they really desire.

Each year these circulating libraries must issue some tens of million books, yet, great as the total volume must be, it is surely exceeded by that of the *Public Libraries* – nearly 500 million volumes a year! As the issues from the latter include a large proportion of serious books – approximately a third are of non-fiction, and in the fiction issues classical and standard literature bulks largely – it will be realized how vital these institutions are to the well-being and progress of the community.

There are public libraries in practically every town in the country and in a majority even of the villages. Actually there are over five hundred municipal libraries, many of them with several branch libraries in the outlying districts, while the county libraries serve no fewer than twenty thousand of the smaller townships and villages.

Some twenty per cent of the population are regular borrowers from the lending departments and many others make use of the reference libraries and reading rooms.

The intelligent book-user must, therefore, take heed of the public library. For one thing, it provides books and services unobtainable elsewhere; for another all its facilities are free to every resident in the district (sometimes others are admitted as well – but see later); for another, the reader, being directly or indirectly a ratepayer, contributes to the cost of the upkeep of his local library.

Public libraries are under the control of the local authorities – i.e. the city and borough and, occasionally, urban district councils for the towns, and the county councils for the rural districts. They are financed out of the local rates, do not receive any assistance from the national government and are not subject to any government control and inspection. Thus every district has been able to build up its library service according to its interest and needs, and surveying the country as a whole, one finds a wide range of provision and great differences in efficiency. Where the authorities have been far-seeing and enthusiastic, admirable systems are in active operation; elsewhere the service may be very bad, and if it is so where you live the only remedy is to rouse public interest and, by comparison with better equipped towns, show what might be done in yours. When you are away from home never fail to visit other libraries and compare them with your own.

If you do not know where the nearest library is situated – and if a directory is not available – send a postcard addressed to the Borough Librarian (or County Librarian), c/o Town Hall (or County Hall).

The headquarters of the county library are generally at the county town, while branches are established at most places throughout the area, of whatever size. At the larger centres there may be special library buildings; at the smaller villages the 'branch' may consist of a small collection of books housed at the schoolroom or village hall. Behind the local provision there are, however, always the resources of the whole county collection, and books required by readers are sent specially on request. Indeed, there is now a national organization of libraries – of which more later – which enables the dweller in the most remote corner of the countryside to obtain practically *any* books he may want *if he will only make his needs known to his local librarian.*

The writer would emphasize this point – applicable to *all* public libraries – that readers frequently fail to obtain what they require because they do not realize the immense resources behind the smallest local collection; they think to themselves: 'It is no use asking for such-and-such books, as they won't have them here'. They might not have them *there*, but, if the local librarian is keen, he can usually obtain them from other libraries.

Town systems comprise a central library and, saving in the smaller places, one or more branch libraries in the suburbs and outlying districts. Excepting in a very few towns readers are allowed to use their tickets at both central and branches according to their convenience. So, if you find it handy to get most of your books from a branch do not forget that the larger and more specialized stock of books at the central library is equally at your disposal. Often there is an elaborate system of interchange by which you can borrow books from one library and return them to any other in the system, as you wish; at other towns, if a book is not available at one branch it is requisitioned by telephone from another and sent for you the same or the following day.

The chief departments of the library are (*a*) the lending or home reading library from which you borrow books to read at home, (*b*) the reference library where you may consult books on the premises, (*c*) the reading rooms, where newspapers and periodicals are displayed, and (*d*) the children's library. Perhaps also there is a lecture room where lectures, exhibitions, dramatic performances and the like are held. Make a point of noticing what is happening in your library lecture room.

Use of the reference library is always open to all, whether living in the district or not. So, wherever you may be, remember that you are free and welcome to use the local reference libraries. Sometimes you may have to sign a visitors' book or fill up forms applying for certain of the books, but on the whole there are very few formalities to observe. The reference libraries of Great Britain are all at your disposal – and you will realize the value of this when you are told that in the reference libraries of London and the Home Counties alone there are nearly one million volumes.

To borrow from the lending libraries it is necessary to have tickets, but these are issued free of charge to all residents on their filling up a form of application agreeing to abide by the rules and regulations. Often those who are employees in a town, or attend educational institutions there, are allowed to borrow free of charge even though they may reside elsewhere. Many libraries go further than this – they will accept the library tickets of other libraries. The scheme began a few years ago when certain progressive holiday resorts, realizing that some visitors read more books when on holiday than they have time to enjoy when working, invited them to use their home town library tickets at the local libraries. Lists were published of towns which granted this privilege – and of the non-holiday towns that returned the compliment; soon some authorities found it easier to accept *any* library tickets. The outstanding extension of this desire to break down unnecessary barriers came during the war when all but one of the London Metropolitan Boroughs agreed to honour one another's tickets. So, if you live in the county of London, you can borrow from any public library in the area (with one exception). Elsewhere, even if this scheme is not operating, non-residents may usually enjoy the same privileges as residents on payment of a small annual subscription (generally about ten shillings).

As a rule, borrowers are allowed two tickets, on only one of which novels may be borrowed. There is a tendency to-day, however, to increase the number of books a borrower may have at once, and to make all tickets 'general' tickets, on which any book, fiction or non-fiction, can be borrowed. And, whatever the *usual* practice may be, very few librarians will refuse a reader as many books as he reasonably requires for a special purpose. Whatever your needs may be, tell the librarian what you want and you will usually get it.

Excepting in a very few libraries, the 'open access' system is in operation. That is to say, readers are allowed to go among the shelves to select their books. The libraries are therefore classified – arranged so that all books on the same subject are together and so that related subjects are near one another. Various systems of classification are in use, but the majority use the Dewey Decimal system, with or without certain modifications.

It is worth while to take a little trouble to understand the outline and general principles of the classification. The catalogues, too, will require some study before you are able to use them properly, even though the method of arrangement may be quite simple.

There are three main forms of catalogue – the printed catalogue, the card catalogue and the sheaf catalogue. The first is going out of favour, partly because it is impossible to keep it up to date, partly because of the expense. In the card catalogue the entries for each book are written or typed on separate cards which are filed in special cabinets of drawers. New cards can be added in their correct places, and obsolete ones removed, at will, so that the card catalogue can always include the latest information. Beginners find it awkward to handle the cards; their fingers all become thumbs, and the process of finding the required entries is a very slow one. The rule, however, is always to turn them over by touching the *sides* and not the tops. The sheaf catalogue is similar, but instead of being on cards, the entries are made on the pages of small loose-leaf books.

Whatever the form, there are various systems of arrangement. The catalogue has to answer many questions – What books are there on a certain subject? Is there a particular book by a certain author? or with this title? What books are there by that author? What is there about a particular person? and so on. Different methods are used to satisfy these demands. Your library might have what is known as a 'Dictionary' catalogue, in which authors, titles and subjects are all included in one alphabetical sequence. Or it might have a 'Classified' catalogue (in which the entries appear in the same order as the books on the shelves) with an 'Author' or 'Name' catalogue as an index. Find out how yours is arranged. Ask one of the assistants to explain it to you.

But, if you are wise, whatever the type of catalogue or system of classification, let the library staff show you where to find your books, tell you what is and is not in the library. Probably you will, when once you have got your bearings, be able to secure most of the items you want without any difficulty, but, if you *cannot*, always ask for assistance. Far too many borrowers fail to secure the best service because they are afraid to 'bother' the staff. A large modern library, no matter how well it is arranged, is a very complicated machine, and the casual user cannot be expected to understand all its details. It is not playing the game, with a staff that is invariably keen, if you go away without the books you need until you have asked for them, personally, from an assistant. What you want might be on a shelf where you did not think of looking; it might be in the hands of another reader.

At every library there are various facilities which may be of considerable importance. Find out all about them. For instance, you will be able to renew books – that is to say, keep them longer than the fortnight usually allowed and after which small fines are generally charged – by post or by telephone; you will be allowed to reserve books so that you may have them next on their being returned to the library. There will be a suggestions book (or forms) in which you can propose that books be added to the library and make recommendations for improving the service. To gain full benefit from the system you should take nothing for granted until you know the rules and regulations backwards.

Mention was made earlier of a system of national co-operation. The most extensive and effective organization of its kind in the world, it embraces nearly all English and Welsh public libraries and a great many university and important specialized libraries. These have agreed to lend to one another practically any books in their collections. The scheme is organized on the following basis: Firstly, the whole country (there is a separate scheme for Scotland) is divided into a number of 'Regions', each with a 'Regional Bureau' and, as a rule, a complete union catalogue of all the non-fiction books in the co-operating libraries.

The individual reader who wants a particular book *must* first go to his local library. If the book is not in stock there his request is sent to the Regional Bureau. If there is a copy in any library in the region, that library is asked to send it to the reader's own library, where he may use it or borrow it.

If there is *not* a copy in the Region the request goes next to the National Central Library in London, an institution maintained partly by a government grant and partly by subscriptions from co-operating libraries and private individuals and by generous assistance from the Carnegie United Kingdom Trust. The N.C.L. acts not only as the pivot of the co-operative scheme but also as a centre for bibliographical information. When it receives a request from a Regional Bureau it may do one of four things: (*a*) supply the book from its own stock – though that was unfortunately sadly diminished by enemy action, (*b*) have it supplied by one of the very many associated special libraries, (*c*) pass it to another region where a copy can be traced, or (*d*) buy a copy if possible and desirable. Before the war there was a fifth way – books were frequently borrowed from libraries in other countries.

With this system it is indeed possible for a reader, no matter where he lives, to obtain practically any special book he may need. This is not an idle boast. At the present writer's own library, for example – and it *is* only an

example as the same applies in many places – records show
that of the books, amounting to nearly 7000 a year, specially
requested by readers, 98 per cent are actually supplied, by
one means or another, including recourse to the Regional
Bureaux and N.C.L. So please ask for what you want. No
charge is made whatever, but you may be asked to pay the
postage, though sometimes the local library bears this
charge itself.

With occasional recourse to the Regional Bureau the
average reader will find that most of his needs can be met
by the public library. He must not, however, expect to
find there an ample supply of the popular biographies and
novels as soon as they are published. It is impossible for the
public library to cater for such immediate popular demands.
To do so it would need hundreds, even thousands, of copies
of some books, and when the first novelty had died down
many of these would be dead stock. The public library has
to meet the more lasting requirements of a public with a
multitude of needs and very varied tastes, and, as its income
is severely limited, though it does much to provide light
reading, it does not attempt to be a competitor to the
commercial circulating libraries.

For the reader who has occasion to turn elsewhere there
are hundreds of collections catering for the advanced worker
in nearly every field of activity. There are law libraries,
engineering libraries, libraries concerned with tropical
diseases, Egyptology, philosophy and practically every important sphere of human endeavour – as well as libraries
on many curious and unimportant byways of thought also.

These resources are not so widely known as they should
be – even to the specialists most concerned. Many of these
libraries are situated in London, but the larger provincial
centres are well provided. Most of them, such as the
University libraries and those of learned societies, are
provided specially for the members, but at a great many
special privileges will be granted to non-members genuinely
able to benefit, others are available on the payment of small

membership subscriptions, while not a few are freely open to the general public. Particulars of these libraries will be found in *The Uses of Libraries*, edited by Dr. E. A. Baker, in *Rye's Guide to the Libraries of London* in *The Aslib Directory*, a guide to sources of specialized information in Great Britain and Ireland, published by the Association of Special Libraries and Information Bureaux, and in *The Libraries, Museums and Art Galleries Year Book*.

Glance at any of these and you will realize how impossible it is to mention here more than a few selected merely as examples.

The largest library in the country and the best known is the British Museum Library, in Bloomsbury, London. Founded partly by gathering together several large collections, including the magnificent library of George III, Sir Hans Sloane's bequest of 40,000 volumes, and the collection of the kings of England from Henry VII to George II, partly by the accumulation of publications received under the Copyright Acts (by which copies of every book published in the United Kingdom must be deposited in the British Museum and certain other libraries), partly by extensive purchases, the stock now amounts to about three million printed books and one hundred and seventy thousand manuscripts.

The British Museum is free to any bona fide student, but, naturally, as the accommodation for readers is limited, it is necessary to restrict the use to those who will benefit most and who are unable to obtain their material elsewhere. Would-be readers must apply in writing to the Director, specifying their business or profession and stating as definitely as possible the exact purpose for which they seek admission. This application must be accompanied by a written recommendation from a householder who must be a person of recognized position.

From the University libraries – which possess between them nearly ten million volumes – the student who can produce a satisfactory reference will also receive every possible assistance, a point worthy of note, as readers are so often under the impression that these fine collections are restricted to members of and students at the Universities.

The same, let it be repeated, applies to such scientific and technical libraries as those of the Patent Office, the Science Museum at South Kensington, the Natural History Museum and many other national institutions and societies. Not even such apparently 'close preserves' as the Foreign Office, the War Office, or the Ministry of Education and other government departments will refuse help to the genuine seeker for information.

The riches, however, are so great that one is tempted to devote pages to describing them. Such space as has been devoted is well spent, if it makes readers realize the wonderful extent of special library provision. Moreover, the spirit that pervades the whole world of libraries is one of helpfulness and co-operation, offering a cordial welcome to all readers and research workers.

CHAPTER SIX

HOW TO USE BOOKS

MANY readers waste their time and energy by treating books in a wrong manner – for one thing, by taking them too seriously and by using them without proper discrimination, strange though this remark may sound.

As we have said before, books are like human friends, acquaintances, colleagues and helpers. With those you love and with whom you are intimately associated, you cannot spend too much time; their company never wearies you, your intercourse with them is ever stimulating. With other men you associate only for special purposes. To some you only go for help in particular matters. Each of the thousands with whom you have relationships, from your nearest relations to the tradesmen who serve you and the inquiry office clerk who tells you what time the next train leaves for Inverness, has a definite and limited function to perform in your life and if he performs it you are content.

So it is with books. Of one you ask 'this', of another 'that' – it may be consolation in time of difficulty, it may be knowledge to guide your future behaviour, it may be something very trivial. Each book must be approached according to what you demand from it.

This might sound obvious, as it should be. But a fairly extensive contact with book-users has shown the writer that by no means all of them appreciate the fact that every book is worth so much attention and no more. There are, for example, many who look upon books only as things to be read completely and throughout from beginning to end, who forget that there are thousands of books which no sane man would *ever* read in that way – and these are not only purely reference works. You may, with reason, refer briefly even to a novel.

Use each book just as much as and no more than is

necessary to get what you want from it, and so devote your time wisely that you are able to get the best out of many instead of the less vital out of a few.

You may read a book throughout. You may *study* it, learning all the information it contains completely and systematically. You may *skim* a book, gaining merely a general idea of its contents without bothering about detail. You may *skip* a book, reading only those passages here and there which concern you. You may turn at once to just those chapters or sections which interest you. You may look at only the one paragraph or line that matters. According to what a book can give you so must you treat it.

You will need experience, however, before you can use books properly in this way. If you don't know how to do it you might skim a book and miss everything that mattered; you might refer to it for one piece of information and not find it because you didn't know where to look.

It is impossible to lay down any rules to guide you, for each book and each reader is different.

The essential thing, however, is to appreciate exactly what you want. Say to yourself, 'Why have I taken up this particular volume? What do I want to get out of it? What can it give me that is valuable to me?' – and you are not likely to go far wrong.

Consider a few examples.

(*a*) This book is a story, not in any way notable for its literary qualities. You have selected it because you seek recreation; you want to enjoy the excitement of unravelling the plot, the pleasure of meeting the characters. You read it throughout, not deliberately omitting any passages, but as quickly and easily as you can, neither concentrating upon detail nor seeking to remember, after the book is once finished, anything but the main features. Your aim is to spend as little time as is necessary to understand what it is all about and if the story is well written you may have no temptation to linger.

(*b*) This is a novel also, but one of a more serious character. Its author does not wish merely to provide recreation. He has written with care and skill, with due regard for beauty and suitability of style. He has used the story as a medium for the revelation of character, in order to give you his ideas about life, or to recreate a period in history, or whatever it may be. The story alone is not all-important. The reader cannot approach this in the same way as he did the previous book. If he gallops through it he will miss everything that matters. Instead, he must give himself enough time, sufficient breathing spaces, to turn over in his own mind the ideas he encounters, to set his imagination busy changing the mere words into mental pictures, to understand what is behind the thoughts and actions portrayed – for every serious novelist only tells his readers so much, expecting them to meet him halfway and add *their* share according to their own experience. Such books are worth deliberate and thoughtful perusal.

Yet, if the story itself is a good one, the reader might find himself carried forward, galloping in spite of himself. In that event what shall he do? If he deliberately slackens his pace he will lose much of the force and impetus of the narrative. The best plan is to gallop on to the end if it is impossible to slow without effort, then turn back and read the novel again – perhaps not completely, but paying heed to the significant passages. How few people read novels twice!

(*c*) This is the life of a musician in which are recorded not only the events of his life, but also details of all his works, which are analysed and described fully. The reader in this case is *not* an experienced musician. Details of the music are beyond his understanding, and, indeed, he is only interested in the *man*, not in the musician. How must *he* approach this biography? He skips it. That is to say he reads all those chapters and paragraphs which deal with the man and passes over those which deal with the music, so far as it is thus possible to separate the two elements. If he attempted to read everything he would find the task wearisome in the extreme.

(*d*) Here the book is the same life of a musician, but the reader is different. He is a music-lover, and for some reason he is not interested in the events of the composer's life (perhaps he has just read another biography which did not give details of the music). He, too, skips, but he omits just those parts which the other man read.

(*e*) The same book again, but now the reader wants to know *only* when one piece of music was written. He turns to the index and finds the page where the piece is mentioned (see later).

One could give other examples, but probably these will suffice.

You will see that to use books for consultation and casual reference you need to be able to find your way about them quickly, and here certain features of most books of information will help you.

The index is the most obvious of these guides. Nearly always found at the very end of the book (though if it isn't, look at the beginning), it is an alphabetical list of the topics comprised, indicating on which pages they are mentioned. Every book, other than a novel or the like, should have an index, though many, alas, are without this necessary key. Other things being equal, avoid a book without an index; it will be less convenient to use, and often the absence of an index is the mark of an inferior production (though not always, of course). Indexes vary in the amount of detail they give. The best show not only the pages where a man (or place or thing) is mentioned, but also state the particular connection in each case.

For example, a full index might read like this:

> Lyndhurst, Lord, Bentinck's attack on, 34; on repeal of Navigation Laws, 127; Marriage Bill of, 134; on Canadian Rebels question, 145; against moderation towards Russia, 347; etc.

Clearly this is better than just –

> Lyndhurst, Lord, 34, 127, 134, 145, 347, etc.

as, if you wanted to know his attitude towards Russia you would need to try each of the other pages in turn until you found the right one.

Some indexes give the most important references in more prominent type.

The following points should be kept in mind:

(*a*) If a work is in more than one volume the index is often at the end of the last volume.

(*b*) Sometimes there are separate indexes of people (nominum), places (locorum), and things (rerum). Don't hastily open the book at the back, find a page with the words starting with the letter P, discover that Peterkin is not listed and jump to the conclusion that Peterkin is therefore not mentioned in the book. You may be looking in the wrong index.

(*c*) There are often several alternative words under which the topic may be listed. The perfect index would provide references from all possible places, but there are very few perfect indexes.·

For example 'Quakers' might be entered under 'Society of Friends', or 'Friends, Society of'; the 'Coal production of Finland' might be found under 'Coal' or under 'Finland'; Mozart's opera *The Magic Flute* might be indexed under that English name or under 'Zauberflote', or 'Flauto Magico'; people with hyphenated names might be entered under the first or the last; people, such as some of the Italian artists, might be under their correct names or under the soubriquet by which they are better known; and so on. Alternatives are innumerable; indeed, the indexer has to list very few matters which might not well be entered in more than one place. Think of all the likely alternatives before you give up the search.

Next is the list of contents, chapter by chapter, found at the front of most English and American books and usually at the back of foreign ones. Very useful are those detailed lists of contents which give the scope of each chapter paragraph by paragraph, thus –

Chapter XXI.

Often these detailed synopses are not printed in the list of chapters at the front of the book, but only at the beginning of each chapter.

Thirdly there are the headlines, printed at the top of every page of most books of information. On the left-hand page, of the open book, you nearly always have the title of the book itself printed throughout the volume; on the right-hand page the headline is either the title of the chapter or even the principal subject treated on that page. In novels and the like the title is usually printed on both left and right pages.

Textbooks, treatises and similar works intended for students often have headings printed in heavier type, or perhaps notes in the outer margin.

Make use of all such aids for finding the place.

The preface to a book often provides a hint as to its scope. In it the author may tell you his reasons for writing it, or his special attitude, his method of approach, perhaps that he has deliberately omitted certain aspects, and so on. Glance through it always.

Illustrations are often placed as near as possible to the things illustrated (though if they are printed on a different kind of paper they are sometimes inserted at places convenient to the binder). Therefore reference to the list of illustrations may help to find information if the index is wanting or deficient.

See whether there are any appendices or supplements.

Remember, too, when searching for information that all books are written according to some plan. If a history or a biography the order is generally chronological; or the treatment may work from simple to complex; or, in travel books the sequence will be that of the journey described; or the matters dealt with will be divided into natural groups and follow in the most useful order. Find out the plan of the book and you know which portion is most likely for your purpose.

Roughly speaking, also, each chapter and each paragraph will treat of some distinct section of the whole subject.

A few minutes spent examining the arrangement and special features will always save time in the long run.

You will also be able to use more books if you are a quick reader.

How quickly can *you* read? How many words can you read, and, of course, understand, in a given time?

The reading speeds of individuals vary remarkably. Some read only a hundred or two words per minute; others can take in a book at the rate of six, seven, or even eight hundred words a minute. A fair speed is about three hundred for ordinary material such as a not *too* light novel. Clearly, if you are reading for recreation or information, the quicker you can do so the more ground you can cover in whatever time is at your disposal. If you read too slowly you are wasting your leisure.

But surely, you may protest, we are not advocating speed? Is it not better to read slowly, paying proper heed to each thought and statement? One would think so, but experts tell us that the quicker the reading the more valuable it is. Speed increases concentration; it makes the mind more alert. Quick reading is not, of course, the same as skimming or skipping. If you do not grasp the full meaning of a passage, if you do not mentally appreciate every word in it, you are not reading it whatever your speed.

The secret of speed lies in taking-in the printed message not in single words but in larger groups of words – phrases, sentences maybe. To make this clear; think of a poster on the hoardings. If it is properly in your range, if you are not too near to see it all at one glance nor so far away that you have difficulty in distinguishing the letters, you will know at a single glance that Someone's Pills are the Best. You will not spell it out word by word. There is only one visual contact, one mental effort, not five. So when reading a book if you practise taking in several words at once you will acquire speed. Slow readers often have the very bad habit of 'reading aloud silently', if so Irish an expression be permitted. They read by sounding the words to themselves. They may even move their lips, unconsciously, as they proceed. Watch a young child reading. This is a mistake. If you are a slow reader get some candid friend to watch you and tell you if you are guilty of this habit.

Such people read by sound, and we should read by sight. Printed and written words should, like little boys, be seen and not heard. This, of course, does not refer to poetry or to certain other kinds of literary passage where the writer is concerned not only with the meaning of words but also with the beauty of their sound. For this reason, indeed, poetry should be read aloud as well as silently. But books on science or detective stories are not written to sound beautiful but to convey facts. Light travels quicker than sound. The eye travels quicker than the ear or the lips.

When you tackle a new subject you may find it difficult to understand, even though you have chosen the simplest available book. Up to a point it is straight sailing, but then you come up against ideas which you simply cannot understand, which no amount of puzzling will make clear. If you are not keen you may possibly give up the study at this point. What *should* you do?

Read on. Understand the passages as well as you can, *but don't worry*. Read on. You may find that shortly you come to something you *can* understand – something which maybe will make the preceding difficulty vanish. If you don't, dip into the book farther on to see if there are any places where you feel at ease. If there aren't you have selected a book beyond your knowledge and you have no alternative but to find another. Frequently, however, the difficult patches are *only* patches; most of the book is quite intelligible. So read what you can and then get another book covering the same ground. It will be surprising how with the aid of a different treatment by another writer much will become clear. Light from two sources will kill the shadows and obscurities, though either one light or the other would have left something in darkness.

This method of study has much to recommend it. If you seek to gain a fairly complete and sound knowledge of something don't imagine that the best way is to select one book and study it thoroughly. On the contrary read two or three books quickly, without bothering whether everything is crystal clear, without *trying* to remember anything in particular. In the end your knowledge may well be more complete. Repetition of salient points will have fixed them in your mind. You will be helped to realize which things are important and which incidental. You will be able to see both the wood and the trees.

Don't blame yourself *always* if you don't understand. The fault may be the writer's, who is failing in his first duty, that of being clear. So try another author before deciding that you are too thick-witted to attempt that particular branch of study.

What about 'making notes'?

If you are seeking information for some definite purpose by all means make a note of it when you find it. If you are using a reference library or consulting a book which you cannot use whenever you want to, let your notes be as detailed as necessary. Don't rely upon your memory and then find when the book has passed out of your reach that you've forgotten the all important formula, the essential date. If the books are always available content yourself with a brief note of the subject and the title, author and page, e.g. 'Mending broken china, Jones Recipes, Vol. 4, p. 201'.

Always put a reference to the book on every note.

If you are reading just for general information or recreation do not bother overmuch about notes. You may never need them, and note-making will slow down your pace of reading and distract you.

If you are *collecting* information for any purpose, do so systematically. Make each note on a separate piece of paper, give it a heading, keep all notes on the same subject together either in folders or envelopes, or at least with paper clips. Then when you want to use your data concerning Henry VIII you have not to sort it out from your other notes on gardening, cookery, next year's holiday or what not.

CHAPTER SEVEN

SELECTION AND CARE OF BOOKS

It is not always easy to select, at your bookshop or library, the particular book which will best serve your purpose, but if, before deciding, you give a little attention to certain points you are less likely either to buy one which will not give you full return or to take home from the library one which will cause you disappointment, delay or inconvenience.

The first – and perhaps obvious – point to consider is how far it meets your requirements. Before you start to select know in your own mind what you want. Go with a definite demand and try to find a book to satisfy it. You may of course wander to the shelves just looking for something to interest you, but if you do you are less likely to spend your reading time to advantage. Go with a purpose, and make that purpose as definite as you can. By all means browse and spend a few minutes looking round the shelves, but do so rather with a view to *future* requirements than to immediate needs. Bookshops and libraries have a way of bewildering by an excess of riches, and the only way to avoid taking a threepenny bit instead of a sovereign out of that storehouse of wealth is to go there with a purpose.

Having made up your mind what you seek do not be satisfied until you have got it. If unaided you fail ask the librarian or bookseller for help. The book you want probably exists, so why take something inferior?

The next consideration in choosing a book is 'Does it cover the ground?' Look at the table of contents, glance at the preface, check up one or two specific points in the index. Does it contain the special information you are seeking?

Thirdly, is it 'suitable'? Is it too technical? or not sufficiently technical? Is it too advanced or too elementary? Is it theoretical when you want a practical treatment? A brief examination should show.

Has it any illustrations? In some books – such as novels – illustrations are a nuisance and an annoyance unless exceptionally good. In others they are unnecessary. (What purpose would they serve in the one you are now reading?) Usually, however, they can convey impressions that cannot be given by words, they can make the theme clearer, and the personalities and places more vivid. Some subjects *demand* illustration. For example a practical book on wireless construction would be useless without diagrams.

Ask yourself whether the subject should be illustrated. If so, are those in the book ample, well chosen and clearly produced? Are they provided with full titles and explanations? Do they look up to date?

Maps and plans can be invaluable in guides and travel books, and in historical works. You should expect to find them.

Is it up to date?

The date is usually important. With technical and scientific books it is vital. Avoid books that are not dated. There is only one reason why a publisher should omit the date, and it is that he hopes still to sell the book to unsuspecting buyers after it has become out of date. It is not suggested that this is always the case, but if the book is one which would soon become obsolete, be suspicious and check it up.

The date is generally given on the front of the title page, but often it is on the back, and sometimes at the end of the preface.

Select the most recent unless the older is the better book and unless the subject is one where date is not important. If you are proposing to buy expensive books note whether there have been previous editions. If so, and if the one offered is a few years old, ask whether a new edition is in preparation. It might so happen that by waiting a few weeks you will obtain a revised edition.

The fact that a book is one of a 'series' should be noted, as it may be a useful guide. Some so-called series are nothing more than miscellaneous collections of books published at the same price and in the same style (so glance through a list to see whether this is so). In a true 'series', however, all the items have some essential similarity. They deal with more or less related subjects, they reach much the same standard of excellence, and most important, they are intended to appeal to the same type of reader.

Don't aim too high. Don't select books intended for the student when your needs are only those of the 'general' reader. Don't choose those giving too much detail – unless you particularly want detail. Don't, in short, take a big book, at first, when a small one is available. You need to be very keen about anything to get through a four or five hundred page tome without your attention flagging, your enthusiasm evaporating. It is much better to enjoy and understand a hundred pages outlining the whole field than to struggle through thrice the number. Moreover, a short introductory work is much more likely to give you a sense of proportion, to indicate essentials and not worry you with details and examples. The short book will probably make you want to read a longer one; the long one may kill all desire to pursue the matter further.

Besides, life is short and, if you are reading solely for general knowledge, rather know a little about six things than a lot – much of which you may not need – about only one.

How is the book produced? Is the print clear? the paper good? the binding neat and attractive? You may have little choice, but when you have don't forget that you will enjoy reading the nicely made book more than one with dirty-looking paper, print that tries the eyes, covers that are unpleasant to hold, and you will be more proud to possess it. Furthermore, the publisher who takes a pride in the material aspect of his wares is more likely to take a similar care about their contents, and you, by showing your preference for the well-made article, can encourage him to provide it.

Since books are your friends and your tools you must look after them properly. With reasonable treatment they will last your lifetime and maybe centuries more.

Yet with ill treatment a book can soon look ragged and dirty, become imperfect, be a constant reproach to the owner who has shown that he does not value it.

Don't mark books with pencil or pen, don't underline passages or write notes in the margins or on blank pages. Make your notes elsewhere, where they will be more useful.

Don't turn down the corners of the pages to mark your place; before long the paper will break off.

You should not need any artificial aid to find your place, but if you *do*, use a thin bookmarker – of paper or thin card. Thick markers will spoil the back and make a permanent opening. Don't use scissors or old letters or anything of that nature.

Don't *force* a book to open or keep open. Present-day cloth bindings usually open easily, but a leather bound book such as you may obtain from the library may be obstinate and have an annoying habit of wanting to shut itself. If so, before you start to read it 'open' it carefully in this manner: place it with its back and open covers on the table, holding the pages upright. Then take a few pages from the beginning and press them horizontally on the front cover. Do likewise with the last few pages. Next press down a few more at the front, a few more from the back, and so on. You will find that the stiffness of the cover has been loosened without any strain or without your breaking the back, as you can easily do if you use force.

Never open the book so that the front and back covers touch. This will break away the sewing. Books are made to lie flat with two pages showing.

If a book wants cutting use a proper paper knife, which should be *blunt*, and take care to cut right into the back. If you are going to read an uncut book it is more satisfactory to make a job of it and cut the book throughout before you start than to try and do it as you go along, as this is bound to prove an annoyance and make you careless.

Never read with dirty hands.

Don't leave books lying face downwards.

Don't use them to prop open windows or as supports for flower pots or for *any* but their legitimate purpose.

Don't let them get wet. When carrying them in the rain wrap them up.

Lastly, never mutilate a book by tearing out pages or removing illustrations

It is often said that books take up a lot of room. As a matter of fact a book-case 3ft. 6in. high by 3ft. 6in. wide will take 180 books of assorted sizes, and this book-case need not project more than 7in. from the wall.

BOOKS AND READING

A short book-list compiled by Anne Cliff, B.A.

The compiler has had in mind the reader who wishes to know more of the history of books and reading, and of the means whereby books have been made available to him. Literary histories, books of literary criticism and literary essays have been excluded. Brief annotations on the contents of the books have been added to those titles that are not self-explanatory.

An attempt has been made in the section on 'Book History' to introduce lesser known aspects of the subject – the fight waged against the book pirates in the Elizabethan period, the book war of the early twentieth century and the difficulties of to-day, against the background of publishing history and the trade's economics. In the section on the 'Growth of the Reading Public', the various influences of the rise of the middle classes, Methodism, the circulating library, and the cheap books of the Minerva Press have been considered alongside the studies of the reading public proper by such authors as Collins and Cruse. The 'Study of Reading' is self-explanatory – what people read and the influence that their reading has on their behaviour and thus indirectly on the community. There is no section here on Libraries as a list entitled 'Libraries: Their History and Use' is to be found at the end of *How to Find Out* by L. R. McColvin, a companion book to the present volume.

BOOK HISTORY

ALDIS, HENRY G. *The Printed Book.* (Cambridge University Press) 1941.

BLACKWELL, BASIL. *The World of Books: A Panorama.* (Dent) 1932.

BROPHY, JOHN. *Britain Needs Books.* (National Book League: Cambridge University Press). Describes the condition and difficulties of the book trade and the growing demand for books in the third year of the war. Appendices giving statistics, reports and bibliography.

COLE, MARGARET. *Books and the People.* (Hogarth Press) 1938.

DUFFUS, R. L. *Books: Their Place in a Democracy.* (Allen & Unwin) 1930.

HAMPDEN, JOHN (Editor). *The Book World.* (Nelson) 1935. Chapters by authorities on various aspects of the book trade, including book circulation by libraries, public and commercial.

HARRISON, FREDERICK. *A Book About Books.* (Murray) 1943.

JUDGE, CYRIL B. *Elizabethan Book Pirates.* (Harvard University Press, Cambridge, Mass.; Oxford University Press, London) 1934. An account of printing and publishing in Elizabethan times and the difficulties with which the trade had to contend.

KNIGHT, CHARLES. *Shadows of the Old Booksellers.* (Routledge) 1865.

LONDON SCHOOL OF ECONOMICS. *Catalogue of a Collection of Works on Publishing and Bookselling in the British Library of Political and Economic Science.* (London School of Economics) 1936.

MACKERROW, R. B. *An Introduction to Bibliography for Literary Students.* (Oxford University Press) 1927.

MACMILLAN, FREDERICK. *The Net Book Agreement, 1899, and The Book War, 1906–1908.* (Privately printed) 1924.

MCMURTRIE, DOUGLAS. *The Book.* (Pitman) 1938.

MUMBY, FRANK A. *Publishing and Bookselling: A History from the Earliest Times to the Present Day*. (Cape) 1930.

NATIONAL BOOK LEAGUE. *Catalogue of the Library*. (National Book League: Cambridge University Press) 1944. A collection of books, pamphlets and extracts on the history and practice of authorship, libraries, printing, publishing, reviewing and reading of books.

NICOLSON, H., ELLIS, HAVELOCK, and Others. *What is a Book? Thoughts about Writing*. (Allen & Unwin) 1936.

PLANT, MARJORIE. *The English Book Trade: An Economic History of the Making and Sale of Books*. (Allen & Unwin) 1939.

RAYMOND, HAROLD. *Publishing and Bookselling*. (Dent) 1938.

SADLEIR, MICHAEL. *Authors and Publishers: A Study in Mutual Esteem*. (Dent) 1932.

SHEAVYN, PHOEBE. *The Literary Profession in the Elizabethan Age*. (Manchester University Press, Manchester) 1909.

SWINNERTON, FRANK. *The Reviewing and Criticism of Books*. (Dent) 1940.

UNWIN, STANLEY. *The Status of Books*. (Allen & Unwin) 1941; *The Truth About Publishing*. (Allen & Unwin) 1946. A survey of the technicalities of publishing as a business and also of the relation between author and publisher.

Growth of the Reading Public

BLAKEY, DOROTHY. *The Minerva Press, 1790-1820*. (Bibliographical Society) 1939.

Books and the Public: A Symposium reprinted from the *Nation and Athenaeum*. (Hogarth Press) 1927.

BOOKS AND READING

COLLINS, A. S. *Authorship in the Days of Johnson: Being a Study of the Relation between Author, Patron, Publisher and Public, 1726-1780.* (Holden) 1927; *The Profession of Letters: A Study of the Relation of Author to Patron, Publisher and Public, 1780-1832.* (Routledge) 1928.

CRUSE, AMY. *The Englishman and his Books in the Early Nineteenth Century.* (Harrap) 1930; *The Victorians and Their Books.* (Allen & Unwin) 1935; *After the Victorians.* (Allen & Unwin) 1938.

DARTON, F. J. HARVEY. *Children's Books in England: Five Centuries of Social Life.* (Cambridge University Press) 1932.

KENYON, FREDERIC G. *Books and Readers in Ancient Greece and Rome.* (Oxford University Press) 1932.

LACKINGTON, JAMES. *Memoirs of the First Forty-Five Years of James Lackington.* (Privately printed) 1791. The autobiography of an eighteenth-century bookseller-publisher, who was one of the first to realize the necessity for cheap books and to promote circulating libraries in the provinces.

LEAVIS, Q. D. *Fiction and the Reading Public.* (Chatto & Windus) 1929. A comparative study of reading publics of the past and of to-day.

SCHUCKING, LEVIN L. *The Sociology of Literary Taste.* (Kegan Paul) 1944. A study in the changes in taste and the reasons for the dominance of a particular taste at a particular time.

SHEPHERD, T. B. *Methodism and the Literature of the Eighteenth Century.* (Epworth Press) 1940. The influence that Methodism had on the growth of reading and on the accessibility of books, and its presentation in literature.

87

THOMPSON, JAMES W. *The Literacy of the Laity in the Middle Ages*. (University of California Press, Berkeley; Cambridge University Press, London) 1939. A study of the literacy of the upper class of medieval society confuting the generally held opinion that illiteracy was almost universal throughout the Middle Ages.

TOMPKINS, J. M. S. *The Popular Novel in England, 1770-1800*. (Constable) 1932.

Study of Reading

BONNY, HAROLD V. *Reading: An Historical and Psychological Study*. (Philip, Gravesend) 1939.

ENGLEDOW, J. H., and FARR, WILLIAM C. *The Reading and Other Interests of School Children in St. Pancras*. (Mary Ward Settlement) 1933.

GRAY, W. S., and LEARY, B. E. *What Makes a Book Readable?* (University of Chicago Press, Chicago; Cambridge University Press, London) 1935.

GRAY, W. S., and MUNRO, RUTH. *The Reading Interests and Habits of Adults*. (Macmillan) 1929.

HAZARD, PAUL. *Books, Children and Men*. (Horn Book Inc., New York) 1944. A survey of the part reading, especially of imaginative literature, plays in the imaginative development of children.

JENKINSON, A. J. *What do Boys and Girls Read?* (Methuen) 1940. New edition in preparation.

JORDAN, A. M. *Children's Interests in Reading*. (North Carolina University Press, New York; Oxford University Press, London) 1926.

ORWELL, GEORGE. *Inside the Whale* (the section on *Boys' Weeklies*). (Gollancz) 1940.

STEVENS, GEORGE, and UNWIN, STANLEY. *Best Sellers: Are They Born or Made?* (Allen & Unwin) 1939.

STRANG, RUTH. *Explorations in Reading Patterns*. (University of Chicago Press, Chicago; Cambridge University Press, London) 1942. A study of reading interests and habits by means of individual case studies.

WAPLES, DOUGLAS. *People and Print: Social Aspects of Reading in the Depression*. (University of Chicago Press, Chicago; Cambridge University Press, London) 1937.

WAPLES, DOUGLAS, and TYLER, R. *What People Want to Read About*. (University of Chicago Press, Chicago; Cambridge University Press, London) 1931.

WAPLES, DOUGLAS, and Others. *What Reading Does to People: A Summary of Evidence on the Social Effects of Reading*. (University of Chicago Press, Chicago; Cambridge University Press, London) 1940.

GUIDES AND AIDS TO READING

ADLER, MORTIMER J. *How to Read a Book: A Guide to Self-Education*. (Jarrolds) 1940.

BELGION, MONTGOMERY. *Reading for Profit*. (Penguin Books) 1945. Lectures on planned reading.

BENNETT, ARNOLD. *Literary Taste: How to Form It*. (Cape) 1937. A guide to readers wishing to form their own libraries: with lists.

COOK, ELIZABETH C. *Reading the Novel*. (Little, Brown, Boston, Mass.) 1933.

DATALLER, ROGER. *The Plain Man and the Novel*. (Nelson) 1940.

FORSTER, E. M. *Aspects of the Novel*. (Edward Arnold) 1927.

GREEN, ROGER LANCELYN. *Tellers of Tales*. (Ward, Leicester) 1946. Studies of authors who have been and are favourites of children at some stage in their reading, and of the books they wrote.

LUBBOCK, PERCY. *The Craft of Fiction*. (Cape) 1921.

MCCOLVIN, LIONEL. *How to Find Out*. (National Book League: Cambridge University Press) 1947.

MAUGHAM, W. S. *Books and You*. (Heinemann) 1940.

MILLER, W. W. *Books: An Introduction to Reading*. (Pitman) 1932.

POCOCK, GUY. *Brush Up Your Reading*. (Dent) 1942. A guide to books worth reading: bibliographies to each section with a special view to their easy availability.

PRITCHARD, F. H. *Books and Readers*. (Harrap) 1931.

RICHARDS, I. A. *Practical Criticism: A Study of Literary Judgment*. (Kegan Paul) 1929. A documented analysis of literary values and techniques; *Principles of Literary Criticism*. (Kegan Paul) 1930. A study of values and their use in appreciating literature and other arts.

SIMNETT, WILLIAM E. *Books and Reading*. (Allen & Unwin) 1930. New edition in preparation.

SMITH, F. SEYMOUR. *An English Library*. (National Book League: Cambridge University Press) 1947. An annotated list of 1300 classics.

THOMPSON, DENYS. *Reading and Discrimination*. (Chatto & Windus) 1934.

Individual Readers

HOWELLS, W. D. *My Literary Passions*. (Harper) 1895. An account of the books that have interested and influenced the author.

JACKSON, HOLBROOK. *The Anatomy of Bibliomania.* (Soncino Press) 1932; *Bookman's Holiday.* (Faber & Faber) 1945.

KELLETT, E. E. *Ex Libris: Confessions of a Constant Reader.* (Allen & Unwin) 1940.

LOWES, JOHN LIVINGSTON. *The Road to Xanadu.* (Constable) 1927. A study of S. T. Coleridge's reading in relation to his poetry.

ROBINSON, HENRY CRABB. *Books and Their Writers.* Edited by Edith J. Morley. (Dent) 1938. 3 vols.

WALPOLE, HUGH. *Reading.* (Jarrolds) 1926.

BOOK-COLLECTING

CARTER, JOHN (Editor). *New Paths in Book-Collecting.* (Constable) 1934.

MUIR, PERCY. *Book-Collecting as a Hobby.* (Gramol Publications) 1945.

NEWTON, A. E. *This Book-Collecting Game.* (Routledge) 1930.

WILLIAMS, IOLO A. *The Elements of Book-Collecting.* (Mathews & Marrot) 1927.

WINTERICH, JOHN. *Books and the Man.* (Allen & Unwin) 1930; *A Primer of Book-Collecting.* (Allen & Unwin) 1928.

FREEDOM OF THE PRESS

CLYDE, WILLIAM. *The Struggle for the Freedom of the Press: From Caxton to Cromwell.* (Oxford University Press) 1934.

COLLET, COLLET D. *History of the Taxes on Knowledge. Their Origin and Repeal.* (Watts) 1934.

CRAIG, ALEC. *The Banned Books of England.* (Allen & Unwin) 1937; *Above All Liberties.* (Allen & Unwin) 1942.

DAWSON, S. A. *The Freedom of the Press.* (Oxford University Press) 1924.

GILLETT, C. R. *Burned Books.* (Columbia University Press, New York; Oxford University Press, London) 1932. 2 vols.

MILTON, JOHN. *Areopagitica.* (Various publishers) 1644.

WICKWAR, W. H. *The Struggle for the Freedom of the Press, 1819-1832.* (Allen & Unwin) 1928.

[*The dates quoted after titles are as far as possible those of the latest revised editions.*]

INDEX

Printed in the United States
By Bookmasters